The FOUR CHURCHES of PECOS

Alden C. Hayes

Published in cooperation with
Southwest Parks and Monuments Association
Globe, Arizona

UNIVERSITY OF NEW MEXICO PRESS

Albuquerque

The FOUR CHURCHES of PECOS

To the memory of

my old friends, Bill Witkind and Jean Pinkley

Contents

PREFACE   ix
INTRODUCTION   xi
I   HISTORICAL BACKGROUND   1
II ARCHITECTURAL SEQUENCE   19
NOTES   67
BIBLIOGRAPHY   71
INDEX   74

Illustrations

1. Suarez's church and the first convento. 21
2. 17th Century church with additions to the convento. 26
3. Final form of the convento in 1680. 27
4. Post-rebellion kiva in area H. 33
5. 18th Century mission, ca. 1776. 36
6. John Mix Stanley's sketch of the Pecos church, 1846. 38
7. Looking down the nave to the sanctuary, ca. 1880. 38
8. Nusbaum's crew excavating the nave, 1915. 39
9. The church in 1891, looking across area H and the convento. 39
10. The south transept after stabilization in 1915. 41
11. Arched doorway from the sacristy into the sanctuary, after restoration by Nusbaum. 42
12. The east stairway after excavation in 1939. 44
13. North wall of room 45. Old "black" wall at left and later "red" wall above rubble fill. 47
14. Cellar in area H. 47
15. Stables west of area H. Rooms 40-42. 49
16. Plan of presidio. 54
17. Rooms 1 and 2, presidio. 55
18. Room 3, *Casas Reales*. 57
19. Room 1, *Casas Reales*. 57
20. A Spanish *real* from a buttress in area H. 60
21. Tower in area E. 61
22. Pecos mission: the pueblo is on the ridge to the left and the ruts of the Santa Fe Trail are visible on the right. 62
23. Pecos mission with the ruins of the pueblo behind it. 63
24. The church before excavation. 63
25. Stabilized foundation of the 17th century. 64
26. Glorieta Mesa from the stabilized nave. 64
27. A reconstructed kiva, Pecos Pueblo. 65
28. View south to Glorieta Mesa across the south pueblo. 65
29. Rosary beads from the convento. 66

Preface

The ruins of Pecos Pueblo and the impressive remains of a church built there by the Spaniards came under federal jurisdiction with the establishment of Pecos National Monument in 1965. The following summer the National Park Service began a program of excavation and stabilization in the area of the mission under the direction of Jean M. Pinkley. It was my lot to summarize the archaeology of the historic structures at Pecos, but I should make it clear that any original work on my part was minimal. Most of the excavation was done by Pinkley and by William B. Witkind for the Museum of New Mexico twenty-five years earlier. Pinkley's tragic death occurred before she could tie down all the loose ends and prepare a report.

Without the notes and ground plans left by Witkind and Pinkley my task would have been impossible—though after rechecking some puzzling areas, I have differed occasionally from their field interpretations.

A thorough bibliographic study, carefully filed and annotated, was done at the project's start by Albert H. Schroeder of the National Park Service. I personally checked all his references and added a few of my own, but without Schroeder's research and Jean's notes this job would have taken many more months to complete. Interpretation of architectural features was also aided by frequent conversations with Park Archaeologist Frank Wilson who was present throughout the period of Pinkley's work, and who brought to his observations many years of experience in the Southwest.

Introduction

Coronado and his successors in the exploration of New Mexico found the Pueblo of Cicuye on the eastern marches to be the largest and most warlike of all the settlements. With the successful colonization of the country under Juan de Oñate in 1598, the pueblo's Tiwa name was dropped in favor of a Hispanicized form of the name they used for themselves, "bÉgish" or "Pecos". Given the reputed nature of the inhabitants, the size of the population, and the location of the pueblo athwart the main route from the upper Rio Grande to the Great Plains, it was natural that Pecos received much attention from Santa Fe. It was the object of early missionary efforts, and the people were courted to provide a military bulwark against Apache and, later, Comanche incursions. Although the decline of a population can seldom be wholly attributed to a single factor, there is no doubt that the heavy casualties suffered by Pecos at the hands of marauding nomads were at least partly responsible for the dwindling of their numbers during the eighteenth century and final abandonment of the pueblo by the few survivors in 1838.

The same route around the southern end of the Rockies that served Spanish trading, hunting, and military parties to the Great Plains in the seventeenth and eighteenth centuries was used by American traders and army men from Missouri in the nineteenth, and the ruins of Pecos became a stopping place on the Santa Fe Trail. The desolate remains of the pueblo and imposing walls of the church and *convento* captured the imaginations of merchants and soldiers, some of whom published romantic descriptions and spread the fame of Pecos in the earliest days of the American occupation. Since the late 1800s Pecos has engaged the scholarly interest of numerous investigators.

Adolph F. Bandelier, on his first trip to the Southwest, spent a week at Pecos in the summer of 1880. He mapped the mesilla and its ruins, both Indian and Spanish, and told the story as far as it was known, both documentary and folkloric, for by that time the small

Spanish community which had grown up nearby was repeating a myth of Montezuma, perpetual fires, and awesome man-eating serpents.[1] Bandelier found there had been considerable destruction of the mission buildings in the thirty years since their description by travelers on the Santa Fe Trail. Mrs. Kozlowski, the wife of a local rancher, told him the church roof was still in place when she arrived in the country in 1858, but that her husband had torn down much of it for building "stables and corrals."

As the result of many visits of shorter duration, Edgar L. Hewett wrote a paper on Pecos in 1904, which, like Bandelier's, was based on surface inspection.

In 1910 A. V. Kidder and Kenneth Chapman, then working with Hewett and the Archaeological Institute of America on the Pajarito Plateau, visited Pecos and collected potsherds from the surface. Chapman returned in 1914 to make a ground plan and a scale model of the ruins.

Kidder returned in 1915 with the Phillips Academy Expedition for the first of ten summers of excavation in the pueblo and nearby sites. During that season the party was joined by Jesse L. Nusbaum who, as representative of the Museum of New Mexico, excavated the church and stabilized the walls with concrete curbings. He also partially rebuilt the rear wall of the sanctuary which had fallen sometime during the preceding twenty years. In digging out the interior of the church about 150 Christian burials were encountered below the floors in the nave, sanctuary, and both arms of the transept. Many were in wooden coffins and at least one wore religious vestments. The remains were reburied when the floor was replaced. Though no report was published, Nusbaum's work made possible the drawing of accurate plans of the church, and stayed for a time the rapid disintegration of the walls. He also took a series of valuable photographs showing the work's progress and the stabilization done.

More work was done in the church in 1925 when Susanna B. Valliant, under Kidder's direction, trenched the cemetery west of the church. Here she found more burials and uncovered a north-south wall forty to fifty feet in front of the facade. Twenty-five burials were removed from the nave of the church at this time.

During the years of the Phillips Academy work Kidder did some testing in the small razed church building a few hundred yards northeast of the north quadrangle of the pueblo,[2] and apparently two or three rooms of a structure lying fifty feet west of the southwest corner of the convento were excavated. No record of this later work has come to light but freshly turned earth in the area can be seen in aerial photographs taken by Charles A. Lindbergh in 1929.

In preparation for New Mexico's Cuarto Centennial celebration Hewett, as Director of the Museum of New Mexico, arranged for more stabilization of the church, excavation of the convento attached to it, partial excavation of the isolated south pueblo just north of the church, and reconstruction of the masonry defense wall which surrounded the mesilla.[3] The work was started in the fall of 1938 by Edwin N. Ferdon and finished in seventeen consecutive months from January, 1939 to September, 1940 under direct supervision of William B. Witkind. Severe winter weather slowed the ambitious project but Witkind completed the wall around the pueblo, re-excavated and stabilized the church, and excavated the core area of the convento. Though no report of the work was published, the field notes, daily log, and Witkind's map are a valuable record.

An important contribution to understanding the historical archaeology of Pecos was the publication in 1956 of *The Missions of New Mexico, 1776*, by Eleanor B. Adams and Angélico Chávez. Pecos was long known to have had two churches but this account, including a detailed description of the Pecos church and convento by Fray Francisco Atanasio Domínguez, raised the possibility of a third and fourth. Aiming to resolve some of the newly posed questions, Stanley A. Stubbs, Bruce T. Ellis, and Alfred E. Dittert, Jr. of the Museum of New Mexico, completely excavated in that same year the foundations of the isolated church northeast of the pueblo which Kidder had outlined earlier.[4]

Pecos became a National Monument in 1965 and in the following summer the National Park Service began a program of excavation and stabilization of the mission ruins under the direction of Jean M. Pinkley. The eighteenth century church was re-excavated and restabilized. In June, 1967 Pinkley, while trenching for the walls of the porter's lodge described by Domínguez, encountered massive masonry foundations at a level immediately below the footings of the standing church. With more exploration she realized she had found the southwest bell tower of an older and much larger church. The remaining walls were traced to reveal that the earlier structure had burned and that another church was built to stand almost entirely within its nave. From notes and photographs of earlier expeditions, it is evident that Nusbaum, Valliant, and Witkind had all uncovered portions of the first building but had not been able to do enough work to interpret what they had seen. Pinkley's discovery that there had actually been at least *three* churches at Pecos, and two on the same site, reconciled discrepancies in descriptions by contemporary observers.

By the fall of 1968 Pinkley had nearly completed stabilization of the eighteenth century church. She had also capped the exposed footings of the one below it for exhibit, and had all but finished excavation of the entire convento, including the slumped and partly back-filled rooms cleared by Witkind.

Jean Pinkley died in February, 1969 before she was able to complete this work and write a report of it.

Roland S. Richert and the writer were detailed by the Southwest Archeological Center to complete the project. Richert completed stabilization of the two churches and the massive north wall of the convento in 1969. In the summer of 1970 I finished Pinkley's ground plans, tested several unplumbed areas in the convento, made tests in the presumably secular structures lying southwest of the mission ruins, and trenched the area immediately west of the churches to locate the seventeenth century cemetery. Stabilization of the convento walls by the local staff of Pecos National Monument is a continuing project.

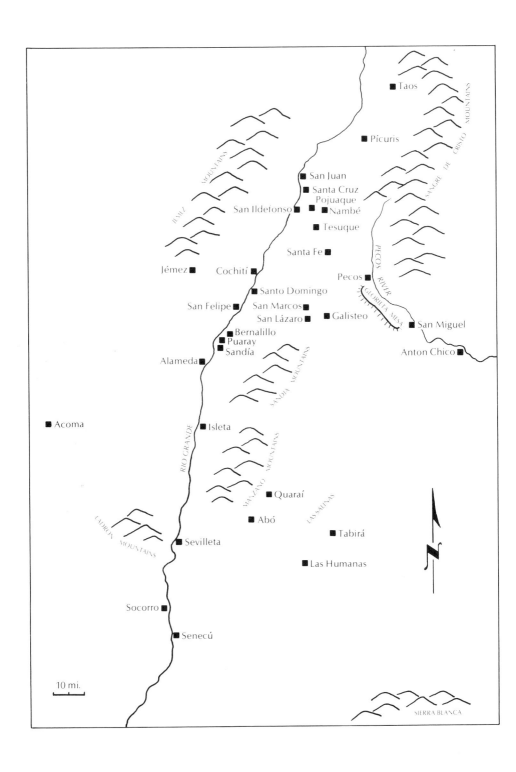

Taos

Pícuris

San Juan
Santa Cruz
Pojuaque
San Ildefonso
Nambé

Tesuque

Santa Fe

Jémez
Cochití

Santo Domingo

San Felipe
San Marcos
San Lázaro
Galisteo

Pecos

San Miguel

Bernalillo
Puaray
Sandía

Anton Chico

Alameda

Acoma

Isleta

Quaraí

Abó

Tabirá

Sevilleta

Las Humanas

Socorro

Senecú

10 mi.

JEMEZ MOUNTAINS

SANGRE DE CRISTO MOUNTAINS

PECOS RIVER

GLORIETA MESA

SANDIA MOUNTAINS

MANZANO MOUNTAINS

LAS SALINAS

LADRON MOUNTAINS

RIO GRANDE

N

SIERRA BLANCA

1

Historical Background

The relative ages of the churches are apparent and reasonably accurate descriptions of each are provided by archaeology. Contemporary documents of the seventeenth and eighteenth centuries furnish both clues and contradictions as to who built them and when.

When Francisco Vázquez de Coronado was preparing to leave New Mexico in 1542 with his army of disappointed conquerors, one member of his party, the lay brother Fray Luis de Ubeda, pleaded to be allowed to remain behind with the "heathen" of Pecos.[1] His request was granted and the expedition returned to New Spain.° Though his was undoubtedly the first missionary effort at the pueblo, it is doubtful that Ubeda was responsible for erection of the small church northeast of the pueblo, or that the antagonized people of Pecos, once the threat of the Spanish army was removed, allowed him much influence. The devoted Ubeda faded from history and may not have lasted long in his lonely ministry. It would not be expected that he would survive until the next party of Europeans saw Pecos, but the remarkable presence of a Christian church—even one in ruins—would hardly escape the attention of Antonio de Espejo who re-explored New Mexico in 1583. But neither Espejo, nor Castaño after him who, with his siege and final

---

°Although New Mexico was part of the Viceroyalty of New Spain (which extended down to Central America), the term is here used to designate the Mexican heartland. In the colonial period, "Mexico" referred to the capital city and its immediate vicinity.

1

occupation of the pueblo in 1590 thoroughly inspected and described the location, made any mention of a church.

The first organized attempt at conversion of Pecos began in the first year of Juan de Oñate's colonization of New Mexico with the assignment of Fray Francisco de San Miguel to the mission in September, 1598.[2] San Miguel was accompanied by the *donado*, Juan de Dios, a Mexican Indian who had been taught the Tiwa language by a Pecos man taken to Mexico by Espejo as a captive. As a donado, Juan was not a friar, nor even a lay brother, but was "donated" by his parents to the Franciscans for instruction and to be reared in the faith.[3] Even with this unusual help the friar's task was a staggering one. Far removed from the tiny capital at San Juan de los Caballeros, he was also to bring the gospel to the large population of the Salinas Province east of the Sandía and Manzano Mountains. There is no evidence that he visited those remote villages, but even if he confined his activity to Pecos he had time to accomplish little. After only six months San Miguel was brought back to provincial headquarters—now at San Gabriel del Yunque, across the Rio Grande from San Juan—in the spring of 1599. He apparently never returned to Pecos. In 1601 he is mentioned as *guardián* at the pueblo of San Ildefonso and later that same year was with the party of deserters which fled to Mexico to escape Oñate's necessarily harsh hold on the fragile colony.[4]

Though Juan de Dios may have remained when Fray Francisco de San Miguel left the pueblo, and may have been responsible for building the first church, it seems a large task for a relatively unsophisticated Indian without any administrative support. For the missions of New Mexico, barely started, underwent a meager decade with a handful of friars concentrated on the Rio Grande and only two or three were left in New Mexico by 1609.

Seventeen new missionaries arrived from Mexico under the leadership of Fray Alonso de Peinado between 1610 and 1612, but the mission at Pecos was not revived until the arrival of Fray Pedro Zambrano Ortiz. Zambrano came to the colony in December, 1616 and may have been assigned early in 1617, but he is first mentioned as guardián of Pecos in 1619. Two years later he moved to Galisteo where he was to remain for ten years. At Galisteo he relieved Fray Pedro de Ortega who, trading ministries, then took his place at Pecos. Ortega served the mission a year before being sent to Taos to found a new mission at that pueblo.[5]

Between them, Zambrano and Ortega spent from two to five

years at Pecos—ample time to have at least started the small church. Evidence that there was some structure for holding mass is found in a letter Ortega wrote to his superiors in September, 1621 complaining of interference in his religious duties by Governor Juan de Eulate. The governor, he declared, favored the idolators and sorcerers of Pecos, hindered the minister's efforts to correct them, and encouraged the Indians not to go to church.[6] Though mass can be said in a temporary ramada, or even outdoors, the church in question was probably the one northeast of the pueblo, for a year later, in September, 1622 his successor, Fray Andrés Suárez, wrote the viceroy that he hoped the church would be completed in another year and asked for a retable of Our Lady of the Angels and other items for the altar. And it is Suárez who is credited by Fray Alonso de Benavides with building the convento and a "church of peculiar construction and beauty, very spacious, with room for all the people of the pueblo"—the *"templo luzido"* dedicated to Nuestra Señora de los Angeles de Porciúncula.[7] Benavides, who was in New Mexico in 1625-29 for the express purpose of inspecting and encouraging the missions, could not have been mistaken in naming Suárez as the architect, for Suárez was still guardián at Pecos during his visit, and Benavides' personal secretary in Santa Fe was Fray Pedro de Ortega, who was probably a source of much information as well as a scribe.

While building his church, Fray Andrés possibly occupied two or three large, heavy-walled rooms at the southern end of the south pueblo about seventy yards north of the building site. The area was tested by Robert Lentz under the direction of Pinkley who determined that they were of Spanish construction.

The south pueblo apparently was not present in the early years of the conquest inasmuch as no mention of it is made in the first descriptions of Pecos. The presence of these rooms provides an argument that the detached house block was built before this second church. Native rooms are known to have been appropriated for use as quarters for the priest, or new rooms abutted to those of the Indians for the same purpose at San Lázaro in the Galisteo,[8] at the mission at Hawikuh,[9] and at San Isidro de las Humanas.[10] If the south pueblo was not yet constructed it would be difficult to account for the large rooms described. There would be no need for them after the convento was attached to the church in the 1620s.

If we accept the convincing documentation that it was indeed Suárez who started construction of the imposing church of Nuestra

Señora de los Angeles in 1622, the archaeological evidence from the small church supports the contention that it was Zambrano—or perhaps both he and Ortega—who built that earlier sanctuary. The excavators, finding little debris, surmised that it had been used for only a short time.[11] Its isolation from the mesa on which the pueblo stood put it in an indefensible position in case of attack, and the location on a narrow ridge allowed no room for attachment of a convento or any expansion whatsoever. And it was far too small to accommodate the expected congregation from a village of close to two thousand persons, or to serve as a base from which to proselytize among the Apaches. With a nave 66 feet long by 24 feet wide, it was one of the three smallest contemporary churches of which we have a record. Only the earlier of the two churches at Quarai and the small church at Tabirá, in the Salinas Province to the south, had less floor space.[12]

Perhaps it was with an exaggerated counterswing that Suárez then built the largest European structure north of the present Mexican border, locating it at one end of the pueblo's narrow mesa where it could be incorporated with the circumvallating wall to augment the defensive posture of the village. It was described as "a magnificent temple adorned with six towers, three on each side. The walls were so thick that services were held within their alcoves."[13] The 133-foot nave was 40 feet wide at the east-facing entrance, narrowing slightly toward the shallow sanctuary, making it even larger than the eighteenth century *parroquia* of San Francisco in Santa Fe. Walls up to 10 feet thick were made still more massive by addition of a series of square buttresses along each side. Examination of measurements given for thirty New Mexico churches by Domínguez in 1776[14] shows that ceiling height approximates width of the nave. In fact, average height slightly exceeds width. Applying the formula to the 1622 structure, and allowing for thickness of the roof and the near certainty that the buttresses rose somewhat above the roof in a crenellated parapet,[15] a total height of about 45 feet, exclusive of towers, is indicated. To a traveler from Santa Fe, topping Glorieta Pass, it must have seemed a magic citadel with its white plastered walls gleaming in the sun.

Fray Andrés, who had come to New Mexico with Peinado in 1612, served at Santo Domingo before his assignment to Pecos. His new church was obviously under construction by the fall of 1622 and it is apparent that Benavides, who left the country in 1629, was describing a completed edifice. Suárez had ten years at Pecos before he was transferred to the Tewa pueblo of Nambé for an equally long stay.[16]

Having confidently established that the masonry footings discovered by Jean Pinkley in 1967 were foundations of the church built by Suárez in 1622 and described in superlatives by Benavides and Vetancurt, it is only fair to cite the one contemporary document to raise some doubt in the minds of historians. An inventory of all the missions of New Mexico with brief descriptions of each, written in the seventeenth century, has this to say of Pecos: "The pueblo of Pecos has a very good church, provision for public worship . . . there are 1189 souls under its administration."[17] This seems a slighting comment when Sandía, which was second to it in size, is spoken of as "an excellent church." San Jose de Jémez, the third largest, is described as "splendid," and San Estevan at Acoma, which was fourth, was "the church which is most handsome." Of twenty-six churches listed, all are credited with conventos except for Pecos and three others.

The document containing this tally implies, but does not explicitly state, that it was compiled by Fray Gerónimo de Zárate Salmerón, founder of the mission at Jémez and builder of its impressive stone church. Zárate was in New Mexico from 1621 to 1626,[18] thus his tour of duty in the field overlapped the tenures of Ortega and Suárez at Pecos. One might speculate that Fray Gerónimo was describing the situation that existed on his arrival in New Mexico, when the Pecos church was indeed rather *"corriente"* and was without any attached quarters for the priest. However, the discoverer of the document, France V. Scholes, found that it spoke of events which had not occurred until after Zárate had returned to Mexico, and by a process of elimination he concluded that it was a list carried south with a returning supply train in 1641.[19] The church that Benavides visited sometime between 1625 and 1629 and described in such glowing terms, and the "magnificent temple" whose destruction in the 1680 rebellion is documented by Vetancurt, were unquestionably the same. There are two references from those intervening years to its having a convento—one of those from the same year as the questionable list of missions. If what is, after all, not a damaging discrepancy must be explained away, perhaps the slight was unintentional but occurred because the list was compiled by one who had not seen Pecos. It must have been the rare priest who personally visited every mission from Senecú to

Taos and from Tabirá to Oraibi. With Pecos in trouble at the time, perhaps it was a place to be avoided.

Conflicting aims of the religious and the secular authorities, and their dual administration of the provinces led to tension between the two groups. This situation plagued all of Spanish America but had been mounting in New Mexico in recent years, in part due to the poverty of the country and competition for its only asset—the labor of the Indians. The governor had to buy his position and neither he nor his men were paid by the Crown. They were expected to support themselves through privileged exaction of tribute from the Indians and by what trading they were able to do. The clergy, charged with the conversion of the native population and the protection of their souls, also made demands on them for construction of mission buildings and for time spent in religious instruction and observances. The Indians, already hard put to satisfy their own needs in a marginal agricultural situation, had to support the entire population while being torn between increasingly antagonistic cliques of foreigners.

Pecos was not alone among the pueblos in feeling effects of the conflict but, because of its long-standing friendship and trade relationship with the Apaches from the plains, was in a particularly vulnerable position. Emulating his predecessor, Governor Luis de Rosas engaged in a lively trade in bison hides with Apaches gathered near the pueblo and enlisted the aid of the Pecos people in furthering this commerce. He was accused by the *custodio* of the New Mexico missions, Fray Estevan de Perea, of promising them permission to return to their old "pagan and idolatrous ways" if they would increase their contribution of hides and woven cotton blankets. In 1641, on an occasion pertinent to our identification of the Pecos churches, Rosas took a quantity of knives to the Pecos so that they might trade with the Apaches on his behalf. When his venture was unsuccessful, he blamed the Franciscans for setting the Indians against him. To the horror of the scandalized natives Rosas had a friar seized and placed under the guard of four *arquebuceros* in the porter's lodge of the convento.[20]

The civil authorities, however, had no franchise on rash acts. An earlier governor, Pedro de Peralta, was arrested in the name of the Inquisition at Isleta, and held in chains for nine months at Sandía where his jailer was the same Fray Estevan de Perea.[21] Although there were occasional intervals of comparative serenity, the seventeenth century was generally a period of turmoil and 'open rivalry. By the 1660s four governors had been excommunicated by their priests; two governors and the wife of one, and four military officers had been tried by the tribunal of the Holy Office.

The two factions were at the point of armed conflict when another incident involved Pecos and its convento. In 1663 a Spaniard who had taken refuge in the church at Santo Domingo was arrested by order of the current governor, Diego Dionisio de Peñalosa Briceño y Berdugo. The custodio, Fray Alonso de Posada, residing in the Pecos convento at the time, interceded and by messenger asked the governor to undo this violation of the sanctuary and to free the man. Peñalosa, feeling a threat of excommunication, attempted to forestall it with quick action. On a Sunday afternoon in August he secretly met his lieutenant governor and a detachment of soldiers on the outskirts of Santa Fe and rode for Pecos, arriving at nine o'clock in the evening. Posada greeted the party courteously and had hot chocolate prepared for them. The governor was not to be put off by such blandishment and asked the friar for a private conference in the cloister, where he threw back his cape and showed the pistols at his waist. Fray Alonso was taken to Santa Fe under arrest.[22]

There can be no doubt that the unfortunate schism in the Spanish ranks weakened the settlers' position and contributed to the success of the Pueblo Revolt in 1680. In August of that year most of the pueblos, in a well-planned and highly organized spirit of cooperation quite unlike their usual behavior, rose up in arms to drive the Spaniards from the country. The latter had scant warning. On the ninth of the month the Indian governors of Pecos and of the Tanos in the Galisteo Valley sent word to Governor Antonio de Otermín in Santa Fe that two men from the Tewa pueblo of Tesuque had asked them to participate in a revolt, but instead they were moved to warn the Europeans. Otermín sent word to the missionaries and the few scattered ranchers to come in to the safety of the capital, and dispatched a squad to Pecos for the safety of Fray Fernando de Velasco. In few cases was the word received for on August 10, 1680, the concerted slaughter occurred. Velasco's intended escort found him dead "near the pueblo of Galisteo, he having escaped that far from the fury of the Pecos." In and near the pueblo, Indians from Pecos, Galisteo, and San Marcos also killed Friars Domingo de Bera of Galisteo and Manuel de Tinoco of San Marcos, Fray Juan de Pedrosa who was apparently visiting from Taos, and three Spanish settlers with their wives and children. The rebels then streamed off to Santa Fe.[23] Apparently the native governor of Pecos, who warned the Spaniards of the impending attack, had little control over his people.

The capital was attacked "on Tuesday, the 13th of said month . . . by all the Indians of the Tanos and Pecos nations and the Queres of San Marcos . . ."[24] After enduring a grueling siege in the *Casas Reales*, during which valiant sorties were made against the belligerent Indians, Otermín successfully escaped downriver to El Paso with the surviving colonists.

While there, in what was to be New Mexico's capital for twelve years, Otermín wrote his reports to the viceroy and listed the fallen, including—"In the convent of Porciúncula de los Pecos, Reverend Father Fernando de Velasco, son of the province and of that of El Santo Evangelio, a native of the city of Cádiz."[25] Fray Fernando, a missionary for thirty years, had been in New Mexico at least since 1659[26] and had served, before coming to Pecos, as minister at the Piro pueblo of Socorro.[27]

Sixteen months after establishing themselves around the mission of Nuestra Señora de Guadalupe at El Paso del Norte, the Spaniards made a foray upriver to Isleta and the bajada overlooking the pueblos of Puaray, Alameda, and Sandía. Here Governor Otermín interrogated captive Piro and Queres men who told him that following the departure of the Spaniards from Santa Fe the Indians built stone shrines in the center of the plaza and on its four sides, where prayer plumes were deposited and offerings made of corn meal. Victorious warriors bathed in the river with yucca root to wash away the effects of baptism in order to return to the condition of their ancestors when they emerged from the mythical sacred lake. Churches at the pueblos were destroyed, the bells broken, and new kivas built or old ones repaired, masks were remade, and the Indians again began to "dance the Cachina."[28] At Sandía the soldiers found that the communion table at the altar, the images of the saints, and the chalices had been desecrated with human excrement.[29] Of particular interest to us is the specific reference to the burning of the church at Pecos.[30]

It was not until the fall of 1692 that, under the new Governor Diego de Vargas, another expedition re-entered the kingdom of New Mexico. Pecos was retaken on October 17 when Vargas and sixty soldiers were met by four hundred armed Indians who, however, submitted peacefully. Fray Francisco Corbera, who

8

accompanied the military party, baptized 248 Indians that day with the help of two other friars.[31]

Although there was no concerted opposition by the rebels, resettlement of New Mexico was no easy matter and Vargas went back to El Paso. A year later he returned, this time to stay. Pacification of the pueblos took another three years and there were repeated sporadic outbreaks. Pecos had played a leading part in the revolt of 1680 but caused no further trouble. There was an aggressive and rebellious faction in the pueblo but it was contained by the friendly native governor, Juan de Ye, and Vargas repeatedly relied on Pecos warriors for aid in subduing some of their more intransigent neighbors.[32]

The military arm of government was busy putting out small fires of insurrection and could not provide the protection necessary for immediate re-establishment of the mission. Nearly another year passed before Pecos was revisited, but in the fall of 1694 Vargas "and the soldiers of the presidio carrying the royal standard" left Santa Fe to escort Fray Diego de la Casa Zeinos to the pueblo to serve as its minister.[33] Vargas urged the people to hasten the rebuilding of their church and he reported their promise to comply—"and they prepared a building for a chapel, which they showed me, with timbers to roof it."[34] Archaeological evidence and further documentary clues, to be discussed later, indicate that Zeinos' temporary "chapel" lay immediately south of, and parallel to, the ruined south nave wall of the earlier church of Andres Suárez. It employed the massive north wall of the convento of the 1620s which still stood over seven feet high at the time of Witkind's 1940 excavations.

Fray Diego, residing at Pecos, probably in restored rooms of the convento, reported to the custodio in December of the same year that Pecos had 763 Christian Indians, and early the following year his chapel was completed. Zeinos had served a total of fifteen or sixteen months when he unfortunately shot and killed an Indian by accident. To forestall further tension with the still-smoldering conservative element in the pueblo, he was removed to Santa Fe and replaced in December, 1695 by Fray Juan Alpuente, assisted by Domingo de Jesús. But a lasting peace was still not established in New Mexico. Another plot like the one that spawned the revolt of 1680 was discovered in March, 1696 by the missionaries, many of whom, including Alpuente, were withdrawn to Santa Fe and the newly founded settlements of Santa Cruz and Bernalillo. Fray Domingo elected to remain at Pecos where he endured the ridicule of the Indians as he preached. Later in the month, Indians broke into his quarters in the middle of the night and removed the sacred vessels along with the keys to his church. He was warned that they would have his head if he remained. Though the governor promised to send soldiers to stay with him, Fray Domingo left, not only Pecos, but New Mexico as well.[35]

Despite the uneasiness experienced by Alpuente and Domingo de Jesús, Pecos remained loyal when violence again broke out on the fourth of June and the men of Taos, Picurís, the Tewa pueblos north of Santa Fe, Cochití, Santo Domingo, and Jémez killed five priests and twenty-one others and then fled into the mountains. Father Corbera, who had said that first mass at Pecos after the reconquest, was burned alive in his own church at San Ildefonso. First news of the uprising was received from San Felipe and a message was immediately dispatched to warn the fathers at Pecos and ask the Indians for help in defending the capital. The next day Fray José García Marín, the newly appointed missionary, came in to Santa Fe accompanied by Fray Miguel de Trizio who fortunately had been visiting him from his post at Jémez. The governor of the pueblo, Don Felipe, followed them on the seventh of June with his war captains and one hundred armed men prepared to help the Spaniards defend themselves. The Pecos further demonstrated their fealty when they seized and brought to Governor Vargas a Jémez man named Cunixu who had come to give them news of the new effort to throw off the Spanish yoke and to enlist their help.[36]

The friars continued to celebrate mass at Pecos—but from Santa Fe and with an escort. In view of the destruction of church property elsewhere and the uncertain situation at Pecos, in July Vargas sent a pack-string of mules and a squad of soldiers to the pueblo to remove the religious articles, stores of grain, and some livestock to safety. He carefully gave spurious reasons for the action to keep his lack of trust from showing. He still had eighty Pecos warriors siding him in the reduction of the rebels. Don Felipe was faithful but hard put to contain the strong rebel faction in the pueblo.[37]

The new revolt failed and the Spaniards held the ground, although it would be some time before they had the military strength to fully re-establish the missions and replace the churches destroyed in 1680. The make-shift church, wedged between the ruins of the old church at Pecos and the convento, continued to serve and to receive some improvements. Vargas reported in November, 1696, "I went out to said Pecos Pueblo and found the Reverend Father who told me that he had celebrated the feasts of All Saints and All Souls—and with the help of the Indians and the assistance of the *Alcalde Mayor* he had added to the body of the church by increasing the height of the clearstory, and to the sanctuary by adding two steps to the main altar, and had walled in the sacristy and had closed the patio at the entrance to the convento with a wall."[38]

In the three years after the abortive 1696 uprising, as many as five friars administered to the spiritual needs of Pecos.[39] It is not clear from available historical sources whether they were in residence or if they continued to make periodic trips out from the capital. The turnover, and the fact that none apparently served longer than six months, leads one to suspect that the mission had no guardián on the premises, but that stopgap assignments from Santa Fe were made during this interval.

A renewed atmosphere of permanence settled over Pecos mission when Fray José de Arranegui was assigned as guardián in August, 1700. He was to remain at this post for eight years. Arranegui continued to say mass in the "temporary" chapel for a time, but by 1705 had started to erect a more adequate structure over the mounded ruins of the profaned church that Suárez built. A status report on the New Mexico missions submitted in January, 1706 by custodio Fray Juan Alvarez has this to say of Pecos:

In the pueblo of Los Pecos, ten leagues distant from the villa of Santa Fe over a rough and mountainous road which is closed during the time of snows and always in danger from the hostile Apaches, the father preacher Fray Joseph de Arranegui is stationed. This mission has no bell, and the ornament is one of those which his Majesty gave in 1698, with a chalice; it has no vials save some little glass vases, one of which is broken. There are in this pueblo about 1000 Christian Indians, large and small, and the mission needs two ministers, alike on account of the number of the people and because the road is often closed and is in continuous danger from the enemy. The building of the church has been begun. This mission is called Nuestra Señora de Porciúncula.[40]

Arranegui's church, while three times the size of the makeshift chapel, was not as ambitious a project as the pre-rebellion church. The old mound was leveled off and the new church erected above the old to fit within its walls with the floor five to seven feet above the old one. Fray José gave it a new orientation with the facade to the west, overlooking the site of the sanctuary of the original church and with the apse over the front portals. The old convento had not been completely destroyed and, with continual modification, served the Zeinos chapel as well as the new church.

The tribulations of Pecos mission, which from 1630 to 1680 were the result of dissension between church and state, and from 1680 to 1700 caused by rebellious Pueblo Indians, were now owing to Apache harassment. These mobile buffalo hunters from east of the Pecos River on the high plains had occasionally been troublesome in the past but just as often were peaceful trading partners. Now, feeling pressure from aggressive Comanches moving down the eastern front of the Rockies into former Apache range, they increasingly expressed their frustration by attacking both Pueblo and Spanish settlements. Alvarez was not the first to record the trouble—two years earlier Don Felipe, still a leader of the Pecos, with his four war captains led a party of forty-two warriors to aid Vargas against Apaches in the Sandía Mountains. This campaign was to be the stalwart captain-general's last. Contracting a fatal illness, he had to leave the field, and retired to his death bed.[41]

For fifteen years there was intermittent hostility from the Apaches. To keep the enemy at a distance, Governor Flores Mogollón published a widely disseminated order in 1712 prohibiting illicit trade with the Jicarilla Apaches and the Utes.[42] It is often difficult to know if such edicts were based on genuine political considerations or if they were simply opportunistic tactics by the governor and his agents to monopolize trade. Pecos was usually in an awkward position because of its favorable location for trade with the Apaches and long-standing associations with them. Although often grouped as a single people, the Apaches were not completely homogeneous. It was the Faraón band of the Canadian River that seemed the most predatory. Their neighbors to the north, the Cuartelejos of southwest Kansas, the Palomas and Carlanas of southern Colorado, and the Olleros and Jicarillas of the mountains of northern New Mexico were frequently trading partners and allies of the Pueblos and the Spanish. Taos and Picurís were raided by the Faraones in 1715 and Governor Flores organized a retaliatory expedition at Picurís in August with Pecos furnishing thirty warriors under Don Felipe's leadership. Although there were also Jicarilla Apache allies, Don Gerónimo, the *capitán* of Taos, objected to the presence of Pecos men. He feared they would inform the enemy of the war party's progress because the Pecos were known to have been friendly with the Apaches ever since the latter "had fled the Pecos vicinity at the time of the reconquest."[43] This distrust persisted even though only a month earlier Pecos and Galisteo had both supplied fighting men for a successful campaign against the Faraones in the Ladron Mountains.

By this time, however, the Apache threat was being replaced by a greater one. In domino fashion the Faraones were being pushed south by their northern neighbors into the Sierra Blanca from whence they continued to harass settlements of Río Abajo, where they were to eventually become known as the Mescaleros. The bands from Colorado, who helped to do that pushing, were in turn being forced into the mountains of northern New Mexico to join the Jicarillas.[44] The ultimate pushers were Comanches, who having recently acquired horses, swept out of southern Wyoming to rapidly become the terror of the South Plains.

The first New Mexico expedition against the Comanches was mounted in 1716[45] and whether Pecos was a party to it is not known. But in that same year the pueblo sent warriors under the faithful Don Felipe to help the Spaniards put down a small insurrection of Hopis which culminated in a fight at Walpi.[46]

A year later a large party of Spanish soldiers, probably accompanied by some of the Pecos, left the pueblo to travel down the Pecos River to Anton Chico and out onto the Llano Estacado for a successful attack on the camp of a large band of Comanches.[47] But ponderous expeditions from the stationary settlements could not contain a highly mobile and scattered enemy, and the horsemen from the plains continued their hit-and-run attacks.

In 1728 Governor Codallos ordered the Jicarillas to move from the Cimarron and across the mountains to Taos. Ostensibly the move was dictated by the need to protect Apaches, Pueblos, and Spaniards from the Comanches. Perhaps a welcome side effect was the benefit to trade of a concentrated population, for in that year Rivera, an inspector-general from Mexico, reported unfavorably on the dual role of soldiers as commercial agents. Many Jicarillas avoided the directed move by fleeing to Pecos to seek shelter with their friends.[48] Apache movement onto the plains had all but ceased in the face of the militarily aggressive Comanches, who were now armed with French guns procured from traders on the Arkansas River in east Texas.[49]

In 1746 there was a Comanche raid on Pecos in which twelve people were killed.[50] A contemporary description of these plainsmen reads:

> Every year at a certain time an Indian nation comes into the province, the barbarous, bellicose Cumanches, never less than 1500 strong. They know no home but are always wandering in battle formation to war on all nations because of their numbers. They camp wherever they will, pitching their tents of buffalo skins which they pack on large dogs bred for the purpose. The clothing of the men does not cover the navel, but on the women it reaches to just below the knee. After concluding the trade which they conduct, which depletes them of their buckskins and buffalo hides and the children which they have captured (for the grown captives are killed), they retire to continue their peregrinations.[51]

Despite the hazards, the Pecos, during Governor Codallos' tenure, petitioned him for permission to go out to the plains for a buffalo hunt. The typically mercenary governor withheld official sanction until the pueblo had sent some of its famed carpenters to Santa Fe to repair his house and he had exacted a promise of buffalo tongues in payment for the privilege. Nearly the entire pueblo left for the hunt but they walked into an ambush laid by the Comanches and many were killed.[52] The Comanches followed up their success with a winter attack on the pueblo in 1748, killing thirteen men before they were repulsed.[53]

Galisteo was equally exposed but the Comanches feared the mortar at the pueblo which could lob stones into their ranks. However, the venal Codallos had it melted down to make knives for trade and in December, 1749 eight men were killed defending the village from attacking Comanches, and a year later two more were slain within sight of the walls.[54]

New Mexico was promised some relief from inept and dishonest administration with the appointment in 1750 of a new governor, Tomás Vélez Cachupín. Vélez found many of the Carlana, Paloma, and Cuartelejo Apaches still living at Pecos and, since they apparently preferred that place to Taos, he encouraged the remainder to settle there to augment the pueblo's defense. Soon a

14

large part of those bands was more or less permanently settled nearby.[55] He then attempted to make peace with the Comanches, granting them rights to come in to Taos for trade. The governor also made presents to the chiefs who agreeably promised to leave Pecos and Galisteo at peace and to quit stealing horses. Though hopeful, he took the precaution of establishing small garrisons of Spanish soldiers at those pueblos, and posting Indian vedettes out in the approaches.[56]

Temporary calm prevailed through most of 1751, but in November the restless enemy struck Pecos again with three hundred warriors. The attack was held off by the ten-man garrison and the fighting men of Pecos who, according to Vélez' report,

> . . . took refuge behind an earthwork and fired upon the enemy. They repulsed the assault, killed six and wounded others badly. They made a second attempt but likewise were repulsed. Chastised, they did not renew the attack, but remained an hour in the neighborhood of the pueblo, a gunshot away, firing off the 16 guns they had and shooting their arrows at the mouth of the trench where the squad was. The latter answered their fire. The Comanche achieved nothing except killing 12 cows pastured outside the pueblo, and, as was their custom, fled suddenly.[57]

Every man in a position of authority has his critics and carpers. Vélez Cachupín was included with is predecessor, Codallos, in an accusation that they had failed to eliminate the Comanche threat due to their desire for economic gain through trade. It was said that horses supplied by the Crown for military use were resold and only the sorriest nags held back for use of the soldiers—at a price—and that for one full year there was no gunpowder in all of New Mexico, it having been sold by the governor to dealers in Chihuahua.[58] Nonetheless, Vélez seems to have pursued the problem with some effectiveness and vigor. Throughout his second term he continued trade at the annual Taos fair, kept Pueblo scouting parties out on the plains, and tried to maintain the garrisons. A reference for 1762 detailing arms sent to the pueblos for their defense includes "one small campaign cannon, three pounds of powder and 250 musket balls" for Pecos.[59]

But the measures taken were those of containment, and were no real solution to the problem. Meanwhile, the low-keyed but permanent state of conflict was exacting its toll. Pecos, at the gate of the pass from the plains to Santa Fe, bore the brunt. The men of Pecos, frequently called upon to provide auxiliaries for Spanish military excursions, were experienced campaigners and the constant exposure depleted their numbers. Even after renewed attempts to make peace with the Comanches, a five-hundred-man attack on Pecos in February, 1772 was reported by Governor Mendinueta. In August, 1774 a war party of one hundred struck, killing seven men and two women working in the corn fields and taking seven captives. In May, 1775 three men were slain while planting their fields and their horses taken.[60] These few references found in the archives must surely be but a fraction of actual occurrences. In addition to attrition from death by violence, the pueblo had endured smallpox epidemics in 1738 and 1748.[61] The pueblo described as the largest in New Mexico at the time of the conquest, and which was still, with one thousand people, second only to Zuni at the beginning of the century, had lost nearly 75 percent of its population in three generations. A census made in 1776 counted 269 surviving Pecos Indians.[62]

In July of that year an event occurred that was insignificant to the history of Pecos and scarcely noticed by the people going about their business of caring for knee-high corn plants and keeping a weather eye open for the enemy, but which was of great interest to historians and archaeologists today. Fray Francisco Atanasio Domínguez visited Pecos and wrote carefully of what he found there. A vigorous, dedicated man in his 30s with the deserved confidence of his superiors, he had been sent from Mexico to make a thorough study of the spiritual and economic status of the New Mexico missions. His detailed description of the church and convento is helpful in unraveling the maze of ruined walls exposed by excavation. He found the church, now seventy years old, to be still impressive and in relatively good repair, but the convento had suffered. The upper story rooms of the western side were in bad condition and unusable as Pecos no longer had a resident father to see that quarters were maintained. The mission was administered from Santa Fe as a *visita*.[63] Entries in the Pecos mission record books in the archives of the Santa Fe archdiocese indicate that this had been the case since 1773 and probably during periodic intervals for some time before.[64]

Domínguez found the people in a pitiable condition. Fields to the north and east of the pueblo which they had formerly irrigated from the Pecos River were of no use "because this pueblo is so

16

much beseiged by the enemy." They were forced to resort to dry-farming fields close under the protective walls and these had produced little because of a drought of several years. "As a result, what few crops there usually are do not last even to the beginning of a new year from the previous October, and hence these miserable wretches are tossed about like a ball in the hands of fortune," wrote Domínguez.[65]

Though there was apparently a resident friar, José Palacio, at the mission for nine or ten months in 1780[66] Pecos had gone into a decline from which it never recovered. Twelve years later, in 1792, the population had fallen to 152,[67] and church records tabulated only 40 by 1815.[68]

While Pecos Pueblo was declining, the new settlement of San Miguel del Vado was springing up eighteen miles east at a ford of the Pecos where the river turns south to plunge through a break in Glorieta Mesa. San Miguel was a community of *genízaros*, Christianized Indians of various tribes, mostly ex-captives of the Comanches. There was a nucleus of settlement there as early as 1794 and in 1804 Fray Francisco Bragado wrote a petition to his superiors on behalf of the people of San Miguel requesting a chapel because of the long and perilous journey to Pecos. Religious needs were still the responsibility of the Pecos missionary—who himself was making periodic trips out from the capital—when in 1812 José Cristóbal Guerrero, a genízaro of Comanche origin, requested a resident priest for San Miguel. The request was granted. The younger village with 230 heads of families, and with Comanches coming in to get baptized, exerted the greater claim.[69]

The Spanish community of Pecos probably had its inception with establishment of a garrison at the pueblo in the 1750s. The first settlers undoubtedly located on the mesilla under the protection of the mission and the pueblo, but in 1825 there is mention, in the church archives in Santa Fe, of a community in the *"cañón de Pecos."* Evidently the Spaniards, who were gradually moving on to the fields abandoned by the Indians three miles north of the pueblo where the Pecos River debouches from the mountains, were building homes closer to the irrigated ground. And in 1827 appears the first entry referring to the church of San Antonio in the modern village of Pecos, inheritor of Nuestra Señora de Porciúncula de los Angeles.[70]

The last entry in the baptismal book of Pecos mission was recorded in 1828[71] and ten years later seventeen survivors, the pathetic remnant of what was once the largest pueblo in New Mexico, trekked toward the Rio Grande. The small party of seven men, seven women, and three children tarried a few days at Sandía Pueblo, then proceeded on to Jémez, the only other pueblo where their language was spoken.[72]

Before leaving their home of centuries, the Indians took the painting of the Virgin from the church and entrusted it to the people of Spanish Pecos. The departing Indians asked that the painting be cared for in the parish church of San Antonio de Padua, with the request that the traditional feast day be celebrated on the second day of every August. This has been done to this day, with the added tribute, since the old church's recent excavation and stabilization, of holding mass in the mission ruins. The people of Jémez, in honor of their cousins, added Nuestra Señora de Porciúncula as a patroness and her day is celebrated there as well as that of San Diego de Jémez. In addition to bringing the Catholic Virgin to their new home, the Pecos men brought some more ancient native religious practices with them. Three sacred "corn mother" fetishes were carefully brought across the Rio Grande and with them the Pecos Eagle Watchers Society and perhaps the Snake Society of modern Jémez.[73]

The last survivor, born in Pecos, was Sesafweyah, baptized as Agustín Pecos, who emigrated as a youth of 12 to 15, and died in 1919. Though only eight of the arrivals at Jémez had descendants, the consciousness of the Pecos heritage lives on in those bearing the patronymics Pecos and Toya and survives now in the blood of many Fraguas, Waquis, Sandos, and Romeros.[74]

II

Architectural Sequence

The first church at Pecos was the isolated structure about a quarter of a mile northeast of the main quadrangle of the pueblo on a narrow ridge just barely wide enough to contain it. It was probably built by Pedro Zambrano Ortiz about 1619. Its excavators found it to be a single nave church, without a transept, facing south, and built of adobe brick on a rather narrow stone foundation. It was apparently used for a relatively short time after its completion, but long enough for a buttress, or curtain wall, to be added to the west side. A small sacristy was under construction at the time the building was abandoned. The church was razed and the timbers and bricks removed for use elsewhere.[1] It may not have been demolished immediately after abandonment. Identical adobes were found in the pueblo where they were used to refloor a burned-out kiva.[2] This may have happened on the heels of the 1680 revolt, as will be discussed later. Building of the sacristy was probably interrupted by the arrival of Andrés Suárez who, recognizing the small potential of the vicinity, abandoned it to locate south of the pueblo.

The site selected by Suárez was at the southern and narrower end of the pear-shaped mesa on which the pueblo stood. The exposed scarp, south-tilting brown-to-gray sandstone of the Sangre de Cristo formation, loses itself south of this point in a plain of alluvium, which drops gently to merge with the valley bottoms. By placing his church here, Suárez sealed off the only easy access to

19

the pueblo in a spot that afforded plenty of level ground for a convento, corrals, or any other needed expansion.

The ground where the church was to sit was nearly level through most of its east-west length. Bedrock was exposed at the eastern two-thirds but it dips sharply at the west side of the ridge and slopes more gently from north to south across the nave, falling 3 feet in 100. Suárez built a massive rubble-filled foundation faced with random masonry of native sandstone to outline the walls. The foundation was brought to level but was footed on the uneven surface of the bedrock with the result that height varied from 2 feet near the center of the north wall of the nave to about 4.5 feet at the south, and to a little over 6 feet outside of the apse at the west. Tests by Witkind reveal that bedrock formed the floor of most of the nave after the depressions in the undulating surface were leveled with adobe. No floor was observed in the sanctuary area but the falling off of bedrock here required a deep fill of earth. The plan indicated by the foundation was of a single nave church with a small trapezoidal sanctuary, flanked by massive earth-fill substructures flanking the apse. The nave tapered from 41 feet wide inside the facade to 37.5 feet at the chancel, thus adding an illusion of even greater depth to the 133-foot nave (Fig. 1).

Viewed from the outside, the church was cruciform though it apparently had no interior transept. What would have been north and south transepts were closed to the nave by walls 5 and 6 feet thick creating two sacristies. Pinkley found traces of adobe brick flooring and white wall plaster in the southern one. Foundations of the nave walls were 9 feet thick exclusive of a series of rectangular buttresses built along the exterior—not as an afterthought but incorporated into the foundation's masonry. Ten buttresses along the north wall were of irregular widths ranging from 4 to 7 feet. Spacing was also uneven, ranging from 2.3 to 4.0 feet, but depth was fairly uniform at about 3.0 feet. Seven buttresses remaining along the south wall were of the same depth but narrower, with wider intervals between them, and more uniform at close to 4.5 feet wide. No trace of buttresses was recorded for the eastern 40 feet of the south wall where this area was roofed to create a baptistry. Maximum thickness of walls, including buttresses, ranged from a little over 11 feet to 13.5 feet.

At the two eastern corners were two small rooms measuring approximately seven by nine feet with walls about three feet thick. Neither was completely traced and precise measurements were

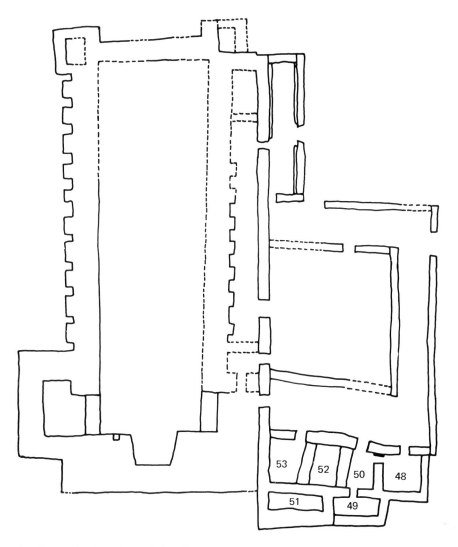

1. Suarez's church and the first convento.

impossible. These were undoubtedly bases for bell towers at the
church facade. Subfloor testing by Witkind in the south sacristy of
the late church exposed the interior walls of the southeast tower
which he found to be coated with white plaster. He also found the
footings of the northeast tower which still had three courses of
adobe bricks in place above the stone masonry. The fill contained
evidence of fire in the form of ash and charcoal and bits of burnt
brick and plaster. Thus, the towers were not solid pylons but

21

enclosed spaces where stairwells probably provided access to a choir loft just inside the door and to the roof. Both towers projected five feet to the east to create a shallow narthex in front of the church. The space was possibly bridged at the height of the ceiling by a balcony which could be reached from the choir loft. The wall of the facade, at eight feet, was somewhat thinner than the nave walls as determined by Pinkley's test below the sanctuary of the eighteenth century church.

Vetancurt,[3] relying on hearsay or upon records that have not come to light, said the church was "adorned with six towers." Outlines of the remaining walls would bear him out. The rubble-filled foundations at the apse are twenty-two feet thick and could serve no other purpose than support of towers—probably at their outer corners if the towers on each side of the church were to be in line. Bases of the remaining two are indicated by intrusions into the inside, eastern corners in the north and south sacristies on either side of the chancel.

Further evidence of adobe construction—and of fire—was found by Witkind in the fill of the nave above the rock floor, and in a test trench cut in the summer of 1970 to the east of the facade. The trench was cut to bedrock and at a right angle to the center of the wall to extend 100 feet east. It revealed that the surface of the atrium in front of the doors was the exposed sandstone for a distance of 17.5 feet. Here bedrock drops vertically for 3.8 feet and was covered for the remaining distance to the bottom of the meadow with from 1 to 4 feet of sterile alluvium. Ground surface in the 1600s was level for about 20 feet next to the church and then gently sloped to the east to drop at the rate of 7 feet in 100. Thirteen burials encountered in the 3-foot wide trench, lying in residual soil below undisturbed later deposits, are proof of the cemetery's location. A lens of soft, white ash from 0.05 to 0.5 foot deep lay on the level atrium for a distance of 19.3 feet in front of the door. Above the ash was a stratum of red clay containing much charcoal, burnt adobe fragments, large flakes of white gypsum plaster, scattered flat slabs of unworked sandstone, and many adobe bricks, both complete and fragmentary. This level was approximately 3.5 feet deep at the upper end and extended for 45 feet down the slope. The greatest concentration of brick and stone was at the outer end. Many adobes, though tilted, were still lined up or stacked in the relative position they would have held in a vertical wall. The adobes were gray to almost black in color and contained much ash, flecks of charcoal, and occasional sherds and bits of bone and appeared to have been made of soil scooped off a trash mound. They were longer and thinner than those commonly used today, measuring 1.5 by 0.78 feet—or roughly 18 by 9½ by 3 inches.

The stratigraphy can be interpreted in this way: when the roof was fired a strong draft was created through the tunnel of the nave from the clearstory window over the chancel thereby blowing ashes out the door. The ash, which was clean and undisturbed, could not have been exposed for long. The east wall of the church must have fallen to protect it very shortly after the fire and is represented by the stratum of charcoal and adobe. Sandstone slabs, found mostly from 40 to 45 feet east of the facade, were probably from a coping at the top of the fire wall above the roof.

Joining the base of the southwest bell tower, a wall 4 feet thick was built parallel to the south nave wall for its full length (Fig. 1). It was made of the same black adobes observed in the trench and was based on one foot of stone masonry foundation. With the south face of the apse it made a continuous wall 158.5 feet long. Forming, as it did, the south wall of the south sacristy it is probable that this wall was part of the initial construction and went up with the church itself, though it was impossible to determine this by checking abutments. It formed the north wall of a convento and created a corridor (area I, Fig. 1) nearly 100 feet long running from the sacristy to the southeast tower, narrowing from 9.5 feet wide at the west to 7.0 at the east end. The stub of a cross-wall 2.8 feet thick and 15.5 feet from the east end of area I was probably the west wall of a baptistry entered from the gospel side of the nave just inside the main entrance. On the floor of this room was a discoidal platform of adobe about 3 feet across and a few inches high which may have been the base of the font.

All of the convento was built after the church was erected, as shown by abutting walls, but the long wall which was apparently built simultaneously with the church indicates that its construction was part of the initial plan. It probably came shortly after the church's completion if it was not started before the primary structure was finished. The first room built was a porter's lodge (room 3) at the east end of the long wall. It was a long room, 10 by 42 feet, with adobe benches 1 foot high by 1.1 feet wide lining the north and south walls. On these benches lolled Governor Rosas' soldiers with their arquebuses, guarding the imprisoned friar in 1641. The floor was of adobe brick and the walls, black adobe footed on masonry like those described previously, were plastered with white gypsum. A doorway in the north wall was reached by two shallow steps and entered the corridor which was at a level 1 foot higher. A door in the center of the south wall led to the outside through a reveal 4 feet wide in the room but splayed to 6 feet on the exterior. A small door at the north end of the west wall entered the cloister. It was probably through here that Governor Peñalosa led Fray Alonso for a private chat in 1663.

Temporal placement of the structures described up to this point is relatively easy to deduce. The church was destroyed by the rebels in 1680 and a new one superimposed but the north convento wall and the porter's lodge were re-used unchanged. But the remainder of the convento posed no such simple problems of deduction. The west side was partially destroyed with the church and these rooms were later rebuilt, some areas were remodeled by partitioning, some earlier walls eliminated, and still newer areas added in a sequence of construction which continued up to the nineteenth century. In some minor details the following account can only be conjectural, but essentially the story can be read through the use of three factors: vertical stratigraphy, wall abutment, and type of building material used. Fortunately for archaeologists, the pre-rebellion walls were mostly built of black, trashy adobes, while Arranegui and his successors used local red soil—occasionally re-using a salvaged brick from the fallen walls. Neither red nor black adobes used grass or straw binder.

The first cloister was a covered ambulatory, 12.0 to 18.5 feet wide, built around three sides of an open patio or garth, 46.0 feet square, which sat against the great north wall. The cloister walls were also built of ash-filled adobe on stone footings but the precision exhibited in the architecture described so far was lost. The garth had no right angles and the walls—particularly at the west side—were crooked and of varying thickness, from 2.3 to 4.6 feet. The wall enclosing the patio was missing at the southwest and northeast corners as a result of post-rebellion remodelling, but the presence of a doorway in the east side indicates that walls originally enclosed the area completely. The cloister could also be entered through wide doorways in front of the porter's lodge and from the south at the east end of the south cloister. Three doorways breached the heavy north wall of the convento in addition to the one entering the porter's lodge. One from the west cloister entered the south sacristy of the church and another led from the north-center of the garth into the long corridor paralleling the nave. A third, lying between these two, entered the east wall of the south transept where it may have joined a passage between the sacristy and the corridor.

The east wall of the garth still stood five feet high upon excavation and undoubtedly the patio was walled to the eaves of the portico but breached with large windows on each side as at San Buenaventura de Las Humanas[4] and at La Purísima Concepción de Aguicu.[5] The floor of the east cloister was native sandstone but bedrock drops steeply to the west, and under the garth and south and west walkways it is covered with up to three feet of undisturbed red alluvium. There was no evidence of prepared floors.

A block of six rooms west of the cloister abuts the latter, indicating later construction, but without these rooms there were no living quarters in the convento so it is likely they were part of the initial plan and went up immediately after the cloister was laid out. The irregular wall of the west cloister to which they were joined predicted the asymmetrical plan of the new rooms. Although there appears to be some effort to square up the walls, there is not a right angle in any of the twenty corners. Floor levels were established by terracing the original ground which slopes to the west with the result that the floors are from 1 to 3 feet lower than that of the cloister. The massiveness of the masonry foundations —from 2 to 4 feet high and 3 to 6 feet wide—suggest that they were meant to support two stories but the adobe walls above them were only 2.0 to 2.5 feet thick. A doorway 3 feet wide connected rooms 49 and 50 (Fig. 2), and similar ones probably reached by low steps or a short ladder, led from rooms 48 and 50 to the cloister's higher level. Witkind's incomplete map shows a door between the cloister and room 53 and it was plotted on the 1970 map in the position he indicated. Not enough of the wall remained during the 1965-70 excavations to reveal its presence. Witkind noted white plaster in rooms 50 and 53 and some was still in place in 1970 on the outside southwest corner of room 48 and in the doorway between that room and the cloister.

This core area of the convento was built as a series of increments but there probably was no interval between stages. Although the western rooms are distorted, the groundplan shown in Figure 1 is a tidy, usable layout that has every evidence of having been planned and built as a unit. Four subsequent substantial additions and a few

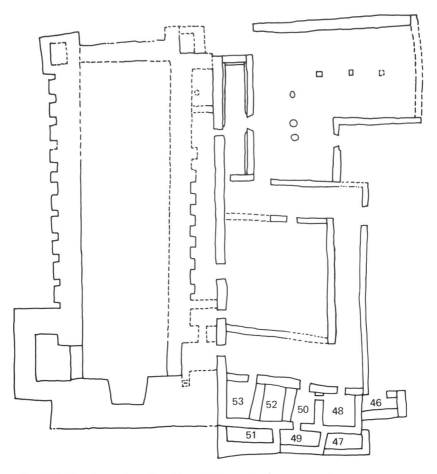

2. 17th Century church with additions to the convento.

minor modifications were made to the pre-rebellion convento, but the order in which they appeared is not so clearly demonstrated and evidence of advance planning of the whole complex is absent. One of the two corral-like courtyards must have been put up fairly early because some method of penning stock would be essential.

The two exterior courtyards had a common corner at the partition wall dividing rooms 28 and 29 (Fig. 3) and met with an abutment that leaves no solid evidence of which was first. It is possible both were built at close to the same time but since the west wall of the south courtyard (area H) is joined to—and built subsequent to—three rooms which appear to be relatively late additions, I believe the east courtyard (area E-F), lying east of the

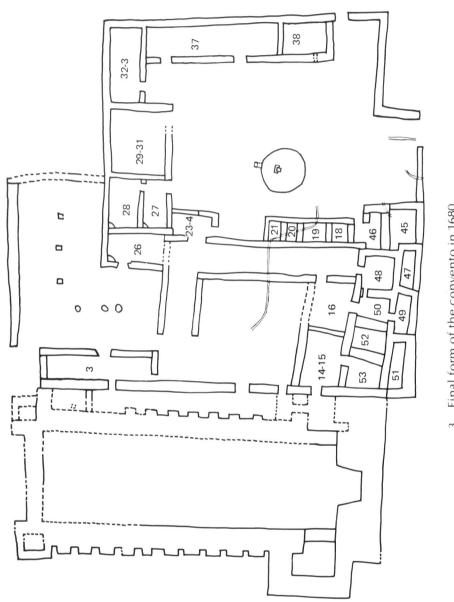

3. Final form of the convento in 1680.

cloister and south of the porter's lodge was the earlier (Fig. 2). This was an L-shaped area measuring 64 by 74 feet. An angled wall joined to the outside of the east cloister was footed on bedrock with a masonry foundation topped with black adobes. Abutted to the south end of it was an east running wall of the same width. It was later removed leaving only the bottom course of stone and was not explored for its full length as it lay under a more recent structure, but it joined the more massive eastern wall of stone, 4.0 feet high by 4.3 feet wide. No adobe remained on either. The east wall was built in line with the front of the church but ended some 20 feet short of the bell tower, leaving an entrance 10.3 feet wide in the side of the cul-de-sac formed by the porter's lodge and the tower. Two rectangular masonry piers placed 18 feet into the yard from the east wall, and three basin-like depressions in the clay floor the same distance in front of the porter's lodge are evidence that an open shed or portal supported by timber pillars once fronted these two sides of the court. The portal would be a nuisance in a corral and may have been added after the second, larger corral was walled in, but it would be welcome temporary shelter for a visitor's mount and his escort. All this construction is described as a series of three or four steps but it is probable that little, if any, time elapsed between stages because until the corral was built with its stables there was not a complete unit.

Fray Andrés Suárez, who was at Pecos for at least ten years, probably saw completion of this much of the convento, and there is some reason to think it remained in this shape during his tenure, for subsequent additions changed the direction the corral faced as well as to make additions to the convento proper. There is no evidence to sustain me but it seems reasonable that Suárez used what he built and liked what he had, and that his successors made the alteration.

The next construction was probably the addition of two rooms to the southwest corner of the convento's core. The combined evidence of groundplan, plaster, and wall construction demonstrates that each was built as a separate unit and that both were built after the convento had been in use for some time.

The west wall of room 46 was erected first abutting against the middle of the plastered exterior of room 48 and extending 16 feet out to the south of the convento with a massive stone footing 4.0 feet wide and 3.2 feet high. No adobes covered the stone when it was excavated and it is possible the entire wall was built of stone.

The south wall, built separately, was a low masonry foundation topped with red adobe brick. A short east wall only 4.5 feet long abutted the south wall with the same kind of footing and brick to leave an opening 8.4 feet wide.

The new building material in room 46, a clean adobe soil, was duplicated in room 47 but did not appear in other construction identifiable as seventeenth century mission. The nature of the fill in this area, which will be discussed in more detail with post-reconquest remodelling, makes it impossible that these were not early rooms. Room 47 was created when the corner, outside of rooms 48 and 49 of the original convento, was closed off with a single wall with bonded corners. This was also red brick on stone foundation. A peculiar situation existed in the southeast corner of the new room. The builders, apparently wanting a longer room than was possible by squaring it off to line up the south wall with the existing south wall of room 48, went past it for three feet to the south then turned another corner and came back to make a butt joint against the plastered outside corner.

Abutments against the plastered exterior of room 48 are evidence that these two rooms post-dated the original structure, and introduction of a new building material as well as the asymmetry suggest another architect or architects. The fact that both rooms flank room 48 but that neither relates to its southwest corner nor to the other new room, suggests they were built at different times.

The walls of room 46 were heavy enough to easily support a second story and its location, jutting out from the south wall of the convento, put it in a good position for enfilading protection of the cloister's long one-story south wall. It may have been a fortified tower built during the rising Apache menace of mid-century. The two-story section of rooms was adequate protection for the west side and the high, parapetted walls of the church dominated the ground to north and east.

At some period after rooms 46 and 47—my guess is between 1640 and 1670—a larger corral was built south of the convento and joined to the southwest corner of area E (Fig. 3). This was built at one time as a single unit, evidenced by a continuous wall running 243 feet without a break or joint from the northwest corner of room 29-31 around to the south and west to a small gate in the southwest corner of the area enclosed. Three large "rooms"—or small pens for stock—were attached to the east wall as it was built. A long hall-like room, 80.8 by 13.8 feet, also fronted the south leg of the wall. This is shown on the map as rooms 37 and 38 but what appears as a partition was in reality a low revetment of masonry separating a "split-level" floor. The smaller area, one foot lower, drained into the courtyard by a vent at the base of the north wall and two doorways led into the yard from the upper level at the eastern end. Pinkley, from the amount of rubble in the fill, believed it to have had a second story—perhaps a hayloft over a stable.

Though it was not attached, and there was a break in the masonry, the seventy-seven feet of continuous stone foundation running west of the gate and making a west wall for the corral is of the same general dimensions and quality and was almost certainly put in at the same time as the longer wall. The walls are footed on the same stratum as those of the cloister—at bedrock at the northeast corner and on sterile soil to south and west. Some of the trash-laden adobe bricks were found still in place at the pen at the northeast (room 29-31) and on the north wall of "room" 37-38.

The west wall of area H was abutted to the outside of the bonded southwest corner of room 45, which must have been there first. Room 45 was constructed when an unjointed wall enclosed the reentrant formed by rooms 46 and 47. All that remained upon excavation was a stone foundation with a maximum height of 2.4 feet with no bricks in place.

Four small rooms, 18 through 21, were built as a unit against the south wall of the cloister with a black adobe wall on masonry foundations up to 3.3 feet high and 1.8 to 2.9 feet wide. These are narrower than most walls of the cell block and probably not intended to carry two stories. The bottom of the stone footings is at the level of the south cloister wall and lower than that of post-rebellion additions in the corral. They were certainly associated with the seventeenth century mission, but there are no connecting walls to give a clue as to when in its sixty-year life they were built. Size and position of the rooms suggest a relationship to area H rather than to the cloister area—perhaps as utility rooms. A remnant of adobe brick flooring was noted in one at a level 1.5 feet below the cloister floor.

Erection of the northeast section of the wall enclosing area H created large rooms or pens. The northernmost and smallest of these may have been intended from the start for human occupancy, but the area just south of it was originally laid out as a large enclosure of twenty-one feet square. It was then partitioned by a cross wall dividing it into rooms 27 and 28, and a doorway with a raised sill of stone connected them. Fireplaces were built into the northeast corners of all three rooms.

A room was made in the northeast corner of area H by putting up a black adobe-stone footed, L-shaped wall abutting the west wall of room 27 and facing the wide doorway into the cloister. The floor level was about two feet below the cloister floor and must have required steps, though none were found. A stone-lined bin against the east wall was apparently a fire or cooking pit and the room (rooms 23-24) was probably a kitchen. If that identification is correct, room 27 may have served as a refectory. There was no doorway connecting the two rooms but at a higher level in the wall than now remains there may have been a "turn" window through which food was passed.[6]

At some time between construction and demolition of the convento a narrow, masonry-based wall was run across the middle of the west cloister and the south wall of the patio was extended to the west to separate the south and west ambulatories. The added partition created two new rooms (14-15 and 16). They were unusually large, measuring roughly seventeen by twenty feet, and their position next to the door into the small south sacristy suggests the possibility that they were used as a vesting sacristy and friar's chapel.

One other feature of the early architecture remains to be described. A series of drains was installed to carry rainwater off to the west where it eventually collected in a tank below the mesa about two hundred yards to the northwest. Drains were subsurface, rectangular in cross-section and built with flat stone slab bases with walls of slabs or masonry of small stones. The longest drain started in the center of the garth where water probably collected from gutters on the cloister roof and led under the south cloister then angled west below the floors of rooms 21, 20, and 19 and out into the corral. Presence of drains in these small rooms may indicate that one or more of them served as a latrine. Two short sections of drains were seen leading out the west gate of area H and another went under the common walls of rooms 45 and 46 into the corral. This last was probably there before the rooms were built to carry water from roofs of rooms west of the cloister.

Though one or two other minor features may have been pre-rebellion, clear evidence of when they were built is lacking and the extent of the seventeenth century establishment was essentially this: a large church and a capacious convento consisting of garth and cloister, nineteen attached rooms, a porter's lodge with its small courtyard, and a large corral with stables and pens.

All this was abandoned when the Indians exploded in revolt in the summer of 1680 and fired the church. Burning out the roof would not cause the buttressed, ten-foot walls to topple, and judging from conditions that existed twenty years later, it is apparent that the vengeful rebels laboriously threw them down to nearly level the structure. The convento was left more or less intact and to express their scorn for the religion of the Spaniards, they built a kiva in the corral south of the cloister.

This series of events was in undoubted retaliation for the stern suppression of native religion, including enforced razing and abandonment of the kivas in the pueblo. Kidder[7] found that of ten kivas apparently in use at the beginning of the mission period, five were filled with trash and three others were unroofed. Only two showed evidence of use until abandonment of the pueblo and these may have been renovated in later, more tolerant, times. A similar situation existed at the Pueblo de las Humanas[8] and probably others. Superposition of religious structures over remains of alien shrines as a symbol of primacy was not uncommon. On his unsuccessful attempt to reconquer the lost kingdom in 1682, Governor Otermín found that the Indians of Sevilleta and Sandía had converted convento cells to kivas.[9] The altar of the church of San Bernardo was built directly over a sand-filled kiva at Awatovi,[10] and a kiva was built in the garth at San Gregorio de Abó.[11] At the latter mission the excavator felt that the kiva and convento were built at the same time, but that the kiva was abandoned and used as a trash deposit from the friar's kitchen. It seems unlikely that the missionary would countenance building a kiva while he was in residence—particularly in that location—but it may have been built during a temporary hiatus in missionary efforts during the 1600s. Abó Pueblo was abandoned shortly before the rebellion, so the kiva was not the result of a post-revolt activity as it was at Pecos, unless there was an unrecorded short-term re-occupation. A similar situation existed in the garth of the mission of Nuestra Señora de la Concepción at Quarai.[12] Though the cases of Abó and Quarai may have been acts of superposition of Christian upon pagan, which was unquestionably the circumstance at Awatovi, in both the former pueblos the mission structures are at a distance from the Indian houses where it would be unusual to find an existing kiva. I believe these are instances of pagan kivas imposed

4. Post-rebellion kiva in area H. (National Park Service photograph)

upon Catholic religious buildings—which was certainly the case at Pecos. The corral rather than the cloister was probably chosen by the Pecos people because bedrock, lying from one to three feet below the garth, would have made it difficult to sink the pit.

The kiva was round, averaged 20.1 feet wide, and entirely subterranean with walls standing at 6.4 feet above the floor without indication of beam seats or other evidence of roofing (Fig. 4). Walls were on a masonry foundation from 1.0 to 1.8 feet high and built up of black adobe bricks, undoubtedly salvaged from the destroyed church. A coat of brown, sandy plaster 0.05 to 0.1 foot thick covered large sections of the wall. The wall was 1.5 feet thick with alternate courses laid crossways. A mortar of red clay was used liberally, so the seams were nearly as thick as the bricks. A ventilator shaft rising immediately behind the east wall was lined on its north and south sides with bricks set on edge and on the east by flat-laid adobes. While digging behind the walls in 1971, preparatory to reconstructing a roof for the kiva. Gary Matlock, of the Monument staff, found an earlier ventilator about 2 feet north which had been filled, plugged, and plastered over.

There were no postholes or other indication of how the kiva was roofed but the condition of the floor and smoke-blackened plaster are proof that it was.

The floor was packed and smoothed adobe clay up to 0.15 foot thick laid over 0.3 foot of sand which had been spread out on sterile red soil. Subfloor tests revealed that the north arc of the wall sat on bedrock which sloped off steeply to the west and south. There were two pits, 0.5 foot wide by 1.0 foot deep south of the central axis and west of the fireplace. The westernmost was covered, just below the floor clay, with a piece of a sandstone comal. A Pecos Glaze-on-white soup plate, of Indian manufacture but Spanish design, lay on the floor against the west wall and a culinary jar sat between the deflector and the southeast quadrant. Part of a Pecos Glaze bowl was found near the south wall and sherds from all of these were also found in the ashes of the firepit. Sherds of three cups and two bowls of polished plain red ware lay scattered over most of the floor. Other sherds were few and the only identifiable decorated ware was Pecos Glaze. Two hammerstones were also found on the floor and a small piece of wax and sulphur, ground and mixed together. Behind the deflector were several fragments of almost completely oxidized iron.

A subrectangular firepit roughly two feet square was sunk 0.2 foot into the floor and paved with a flagstone hearth. At the rear of the pit, at floor level, was an ashpit the width of the firepit and 0.8 foot deep flanked by sheltering arms of adobe terraced up from 0.2 foot high at the outer ends to 0.5 where they joined the deflector. The latter, 3.5 feet wide by 3.0 feet high and 0.8 foot thick, was built of adobe bricks. It rose in three terraces to make a cloud-altar shape. Both firepit and ash-shelf were filled and piled high with white ash which spilled over the arms of the altar and onto the floor. In the ash were numerous strips of muscovite mica cut into long rectangles, and a quantity of broken and charred food bones, including those of a domestic rooster (identified by Charmion R. McKusick).

The kiva was filled with remarkably clean soil containing little cultural material and no wood. The impression was that it was deliberately back-filled. Only 111 sherds came from the fill. Seventeen of the 24 identifiable decorated sherds were Pecos Glaze but they included several Kapo Black and polished redware sherds, and one Tewa Polychrome. The remaining inventory was: a large piece of split selenite, a cut mica disk, two chalcedony edge-scrapers, one sherd of dark green bottle glass, and a thick fragment of a bronze bell. It would be interesting to know how this last compares with eight pieces found by Kidder in the main pueblo, three excavated by John Corbett in the South Mound, and those reported from Glorieta Mesa by Bandelier.

When Vargas escorted Fray Diego de la Casa Zeinos to Pecos during the reconquest of New Mexico from El Paso del Norte, they found a low mound of rubble and melted adobe where the church had stood. The roofs and upper wall of the western rooms of the convento were missing and this may have been true of many others, but the great north wall was largely intact. Some rooms, in addition to the kiva, may have been occupied by Indians with or without remodelling, as was true of Awatovi and Hawikuh.[13]

For the temporary chapel referred to by Vargas, Zeinos levelled off the rubble of the south nave wall of the razed church and built three walls of a structure against the north side of the long convento wall. There is no archaeological evidence for the chapel beyond the fact that Witkind found five adolescent, Christian burials below the floor of the east end of area I, and an unrecorded number were encountered by Pinkley. Burial within the nave of a church was a common practice and, while they did occur in the convento, they were few, scattered, and mostly relatively recent. But we have Vargas' word that there *was* a chapel before the church was built and the description left by Domínguez identifies it as our area I. The small, "temporary" church was in use for nine years and in 1696 underwent some alterations and additions. In that year, according to Vargas, "the Reverend Father—had walled in the sacristy and had closed the patio at the entrance to the convento with a wall." This last undoubtedly refers to the opening in the northeast corner of area F, which was closed when the south wall of room 1 was put up of red adobes on a stone foundation (Fig. 5). There must have been other work done in the convento during the period when Zeinos' little church was in use, but it is not possible to say exactly when between 1694 and the late 1700s most of the modifications were made.

Counting the little church just discussed, the more permanent structure begun by Fray José de Arranegui by 1705 was the fourth church at Pecos. A much less imposing building than the pre-revolt church, it was built on the mounded rubble of the latter in a

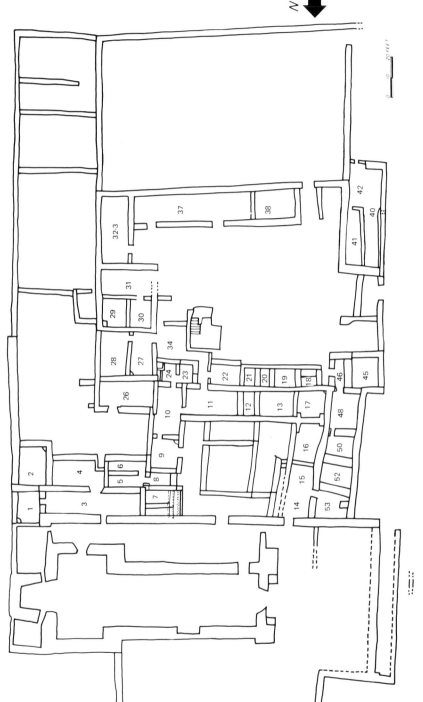

5. 18th Century mission, ca. 1776.

cruciform with an open transept and a reversed orientation. The rear wall of the apse was built over the narthex of the first church and the west-facing door did not reach to the old chancel. Walls of red adobe from 5.0 to 6.2 feet thick enclosed a nave 76 feet long. Walls of the transept and apse, which of course were somewhat higher to allow for a clearstory, were thicker and ran from 5.5 to 7.5 feet. The area once occupied by the apse and four western bell towers of the earlier church became the cemetery for the later one. The western wall of the cemetery was built above the 6-foot-high foundations of the old apse, which remained a terrace above the land sloping west into Arroyo del Pueblo. The cemetery's north wall tied to the corner of the west, to run east for a short distance then jogged north to join the defense wall encircling the pueblo. An east wall ran from the latter to the west corner of the north transept of the church to make an L-shaped, combined *campo santo*, atrium, and courtyard.

Two bell towers flanked the door to make a shallow narthex. It held a balcony which Domínguez tells us was entered through a window from the choir loft. A line drawing from field sketches by John Mix Stanly of Lt. W. H. Emory's party in 1846[14] shows the wooden balustrade in place and towers still standing (Fig. 6). The quotes that follow are from the account of Fray Francisco Atanasio Domínguez,[15] which supplies many missing details and is helpful in identifying eroded archaeological features. Of the towers he says: "On top of the flat roof at both front corners there are two small towers with a small bell donated by the King in one of them. . . ."

Evidence of roofing must come from Domínguez and from old photographs. Beams were squared timbers set on two-foot centers and rested at the ends on carved corbels. The roof over the transept and sanctuary was higher and provided for a grilled clearstory window (Fig. 7).

Fenestration was rather elaborate for a New Mexico church. In addition to light shed on the sanctuary from the clearstory, the transept was lit by a large window high in its north wall which Domínguez found barred "with a wooden grating." After his visit it was plugged at the back with adobe bricks to form a large, high niche (Fig. 8). Strangely, Fray Francisco did not note a similar opening in the north nave wall, which appears in a photograph taken about 1891 (Fig. 9), but he mentions "three windows facing south on the Epistle side of the nave." These would look out over the roof of area I.

6. John Mix Stanley's sketch of the Pecos church, 1846.

7. Looking down the nave to the sanctuary, ca. 1880. (Museum of New Mexico photograph)

8. Nusbaum's crew excavating the nave, 1915. (Museum of New Mexico photograph)

9. The church in 1891, looking across area H and the convento. (Museum of New Mexico photograph)

"A seemly tribune" in the south transept was a balcony 17 to 18 feet above the floor. Timbers still in position in 1915 indicate that it was about eight feet wide and lined the south and east walls of the transept (Fig. 10). It was entered through a high door leading out onto the roof of area I, Zeinos' old church.

The 1776 account describes the altar with five steps of hewn timbers leading to it and with two oil paintings, donated by the king, on the wall behind. They were of Our Lady of the Assumption and Nuestra Señora de los Angeles. One survives in the church of San Antonio de Padua in the modern village of Pecos, where it was left by the departing Indians in 1838.

There were also side altars in both arms of the transept.

> The one on the Gospel side [north] is at the end wall under the window mentioned above. It is dedicated to St. Anthony of Padua, whose image is an ordinary, fairly good painting on buffalo skin. The other altar is under the above mentioned tribune. It is dedicated to Our Lady of Guadalupe with a painting on buffalo skin like the above.

There was a "wooden pulpit in the usual place"—this would be against the south nave wall next to the transept. Domínguez does not refer to a large nich near the middle of the north nave wall as such but *does* say, "there is a pretty wooden confessional on a platform on the Gospel side and then a long bench with legs." It is possible that a confessional, fronted with wood, was set back into the niche, which is 11 feet long by 3.5 feet deep. The lintel, missing by 1915, appears in old photographs as a squared timber let back into the bricks of the wall and appears to be about seven feet above the floor (Figs. 8 and 10).

At one time there was a small doorway in the south nave wall near the transept in the vicinity of the pulpit. This access had apparently been obliterated by the time of Domínguez' inspection. Although no trace of the doorway remains now, we can see from a 1911 photograph in the Museum of New Mexico archives that it was a true arch, blocked at the nave side of the wall to form a deep niche or cubby.

There also were small arched doorways at the top of the altar steps, at each side of the front of the sanctuary (Fig. 11). The one to the north, above which was hung "an old middle-sized oil painting on canvas of Jesús Nazareno," led into a "little room for the storing of church belongings." Witkind found several infant burials below

10. The south transept after stabilization in 1915. (Museum of New Mexico photograph)

the floor here. The opposite door led into the sacristy and above it was a painting "on buffalo skin and so old that the image is undistinguishable." Arches are rare in New Mexico's adobe architecture—these three being the only ones known in a church interior—but arches were used in the portal or porter's lodge to the old convento at Isleta Pueblo, and in bell towers at San Ildefonso, San Juan, and Pojoaque.[16] Though Nusbaum reconstructed two sanctuary doors as true arches with a keystone of adobe brick, his prestabilization pictures show that, unlike the arched door in the nave, these were primitive arches made by extending each successive layer of bricks a few inches out into the doorway and then trimming and plastering for the rounded effect.

The sacristy was built by walling in the re-entrant corner between the apse and south transept—the south wall joining the end of the old pre-revolt "great north wall" of the convento. In addition to access from the sanctuary, a small door led into area I between the convento and the south nave wall. Domínguez

11. Arched doorway from the sacristy into the sanctuary, after restoration by Nusbaum. (Helga Teiwes, Arizona State Museum)

describes in detail the furnishings and items pertaining to worship that were kept there, and a "window to the south on one side." This must have been high in the wall to look over the lower roof level of room 1.

The convento saw considerable alteration and some additions. Some partition walls put in after the return of the missionaries were removed before Domínguez' visit about seventy years later, while others were added by teamsters and herders after his time—and even after the mission's abandonment. It is impossible to determine a relative placement in time for many walls, but a reasonable deduction can be made for others. In several areas it is fairly certain that rebuilding was done in the years encompassed by the tenures of Zeinos and Arranegui—about 1694 to 1708.

Essentially all post-rebellion construction was done with the same clean, red adobe that was used in the eighteenth century church, and we saw a switch to this material with the late addition to the first convento—room 47. However, some obviously later walls with or without stone footings, built on accumulated fill, were made of black adobes or a mixture of the two kinds. This later building with trash-filled bricks was almost certainly done with brick salvaged from the rubble left over from the 1680 uprising. Therefore this construction must have been relatively early after the reconquest while old bricks were still available.

One early remodelling job was the constriction of the cloister area to less than a quarter of its original size by partitioning the ambulatory into ten rooms and by building a new wall inside the old patio to make cloister walks in what was once the outer edges of the garth. The garth walls were built of red and black adobes on two feet of stone foundation. Upon excavation the walls were at no spot as much as three feet high but Domínguez says of them, "the lower cloister is enclosed, with two windows on each side making eight in all." The open patio was paved with flagstones. For a time the four-sided cloister probably permitted passage completely around the patio. But before Domínguez' inspection it was cut up, when a stone masonry footing on fill divided the west from the south ambulatory, and walls of red and of mixed black and red adobes placed directly on earth fill without foundations were built at the southeast and northwest corners of the garth. The only open walkway then was at the east and north sides. Witkind reported an adobe brick floor under the north cloister and gypsum plaster on the walls.

The original south and east cloisters were divided into ten rooms by erecting partitions of adobe bricks on earth fill from 0.5 foot to 2.4 feet above the original floors. All remaining walls were of black adobes except for the partition dividing rooms 9 and 10 which contained both black and red—some of them burned. Floors of adobe brick were laid in rooms 9 and 11 and traces of white plaster remained in rooms 9 and 10. Fireplaces were built into the southwest corners of rooms 9 and 17.

The doorway leading from the old cloister into the east courtyard was narrowed, when room 8 was built, by laying up jambs of red adobe abutting the black bricks of the original walls and the door in the south wall of room 10—originally an exit into the south courtyard—was also partially plugged. The south end of the east wall of room 10 was apparently knocked out in the 1680 troubles and rebuilt one foot west of its initial placement with new masonry footings and a mixture of red and black adobes.

12. The east stairway after excavation in 1939. (Erik Reed photograph)

A flight of stairs, 12 feet wide at the bottom west of room 7, and narrowing to 7.0 feet, was built at the northeast corner of the cloister to rise to the east and to terminate at the east end of the roof of room 3 (Fig. 12). Heavy, squared timbers were used as risers which fronted treads of earth fill. The lower three long risers were inserted in holes cut into the adobe of flanking walls. The south ends of the shorter risers rested on the north wall of room 7, a low closet.

There was more extensive shifting of walls west of the cloister. The south end of the thick wall forming the west side of the seventeenth century garth was destroyed and was replaced 4.8 feet to the west when a stone foundation on 1.6 feet of rubble fill was topped with black bricks. Overlapping of new and old walls (east side of rooms 14 and 15), made an almost bastion-like footing 8 feet thick, more than enough to hold up the second story. The buttresses seen at each end of the wall dividing rooms 16 and 17 were undoubtedly for that purpose. With the first convento this wall had only to support the cloister roof, but was possibly not stout enough to hold the weight of the second story walls which we know from Domínguez existed there in the 1700s. The wall had apparently fallen down to the stone foundation and debris on the floor was leveled off at that height—about 1.6 feet above the old floor—and the short buttresses of masonry were laid across the foundation against the east and west walls. The one at the west overlapped the plugged doorway between rooms 17 and 48.

There were still more alterations on this area. The north wall of room 16 was also razed down to the masonry footing. It was rebuilt on fill and without stone just above the old foundation and 1.8 feet to the south. The large room north of this wall was then divided by a similar wall to create rooms 14 and 15. The partition was removed—totally at the west end, and to only one brick high and covered with a new floor level for the rest of its length—probably before the Domínguez visit.

A second area of early reconstruction was in convento rooms west of the old cloister. These were in bad condition with roofs and upper sections of the walls having collapsed. The three outer rooms, 47, 49 and 51, were probably never rebuilt. Very little adobe remained on the foundations when they were excavated in 1966-67, they were not found by Witkind, and are omitted from Fray Francisco's description. By that time they were probably buried under a sloping talus against the west walls of the four rooms east of them. When the mission was reoccupied, the black adobe walls of these rooms still stood from 1.7 to 5.4 feet high. They were raised to desired height by addition of red adobe bricks. The changed pattern of abutted and bonded corners shown in Figures 3 and 5 is a reflection of rebuilding. The *early* south wall of room 52 was abutted to the west but the raised courses of red bricks were tied, and the south wall of room 50—once bonded—was abutted at the higher level. New floor levels were established over a deposit of broken bricks, charcoal, ash, and bits of white plaster.

Witkind excavated these rooms in 1940 and his notes on room 50 (his room 13) are particularly interesting. He found the east wall still standing about eight feet high. He went through timbers he believed to be from the roof and then encountered another layer of wood he judged to be the sagged floor of a second story. This floor could be traced only across the south half of the room and was lined at its north edge by a low adobe wall three courses high. Near the middle of the east wall and against it were three large posts planted vertically. He reported white plaster on the south wall but none on the north. In light of the Domínguez account, which was not available to Witkind, I believe the missing north half of the second floor was occupied by a stairway supported by the vertical timbers. The low wall of adobe may have been what was left of a protective banister above the open well.

In room 48 the original black, south wall stood only 1.6 feet high. It was capped with two courses of red bricks and fallen rubble in the room was leveled off at the top of these bricks to make a new floor. A new south wall was erected just outside of the old. It abutted the odd southeast, outside corner of room 47, crossed 4.1 feet of adobe fill in room 45 (Fig. 13) and the north end of the thick masonry wall separating rooms 45 and 46, and crossed similar rubble fill in room 45 to abut the west end of the south wall of the original south cloister. A fireplace was built in the southwest corner of room 48 on top of the truncated first south wall. A door was cut in the south wall, where none had existed, to lead into room 46. Open doors from rooms 48 and 50 leading to rooms 17 and 16 were plugged with red adobe bricks.

A third area of added construction which can be dated with some certainty consists of more corrals to the south of those which already existed. A large pen, area G, 73 by 123 feet, was added south of area H. The walls at the time of their excavation stood to a maximum height of 4.8 feet and were entirely of stone. The south wall of area E, the entry courtyard for the seventeenth century convento was completely removed, probably shortly after the rebellion, and the area covered with alluvium of melted adobes from the ruins to a depth of a little over 2 feet. The east wall of area E-F, in line with the front of the old church, was capped over several inches of alluvium with more stone and was extended south to turn and abut the southeast corner of the new large corral. It was then subdivided into four pens. The new stock pens (areas B, C and D) may have been associated with the emphasis on trade with the Plains Indians that characterized the mid-1700s. Though the larger corral, area G, may possibly have been built prior to the rebellion, areas B, C and D are definitely a later period. In area F, four new rooms (2, 4-6) were added in front of the old porter's lodge where the open portico once stood.

In the northeast corner of area H, just east of the kiva, a cellar was dug about 6.5 feet deep (Fig. 14). It was lined and paved with

13. North wall of room 45. Old "black" wall at left and later "red" wall above rubble fill. (National Park Service photograph)

14. Cellar in area H. (National Park Service photograph)

black adobe bricks and the walls were whitewashed. It was entered from the south by means of seven adobe steps. There were no remains of roofing material nor any evidence of how it was roofed. Apparently it had been backfilled.

Although the cellar was lined entirely with black adobes in the style of the early convento, I believe it was built shortly after the reconquest out of salvaged bricks. A stone foundation topped with red adobes was built immediately above the subterranean east wall of the cellar, and a red adobe wall without any stone above the north wall. Pinkley's map suggests that there were once similar walls to the south and west which no longer remained in 1970. In that year the remnant walls stood a maximum of 2.6 feet above the surface. The cellar may have been roofed across these walls to show a low profile above the corral floor. Witkind's log mentions the possible remains of a kiva or defensive tower in this vicinity. Abutted to the north and east walls was a black adobe wall on accumulated fill and a red brick wall on a stone footing which created rooms 22 and 34 respectively, and a passage from the latter to room 11 in the convento. This construction is typical of post-revolt building and certainly related to the cellar. If the cellar preceded the above-ground walls by an appreciable length of time it was floating free in the corral instead of occupying a more likely position next to the south wall of the convento or nested in the corner next to the kitchen. Another hint that it may have been Zeinos' work in the late 1690s is the sterile nature of the fill in the kiva immediately to the west. Earth from the cellar probably filled the kiva and it is sure that the minister would not tolerate for long this defiant symbol of paganism.

In this same area the small kitchen was made into two rooms (23-4) by a short divider wall, and above the firepit in the original floor a raised cooking platform, about 30 inches high, was built of earth fill behind a front of stone masonry.

One more addition in the area of the corrals, probably post-revolt but impossible to date any closer, was the creation of rooms 40 through 42 south of the west gate of area H. This was given three room numbers because of a low wall of rubble masonry which appeared to divide the area. It was all, in fact, one enclosure (Fig. 15). The east half of the floor was paved with cobblestones neatly placed on their narrower edges above 0.2 foot of rotted organic matter. The west half of the floor sat at a level about 0.6 foot lower and was covered with several inches of the same fine, yellow-green

15. Stables west of area H. Rooms 40-42. (National Park Service photograph)

organic matter. South of the low dividing wall were two long poles laid to make a continuation of it. A series of juniper poles an estimated 0.2 to 0.3 foot in original diameter lay east-west across the west half of the room. Original spacing seems to have been about 1.5 feet apart. The butts of the small poles lay above the heavier north-south poles at the south end of the room while those in the vicinity of the rubble wall were, in some cases, imbedded in the stone. Two small post-molds were found along the line of juniper butts. The longest remaining pole was 8.8 feet. Along the foot of the north half of the west wall was a shallow trench terminating in an open drain under the wall. The only entrance was a doorway in the south wall leading to open country outside the convento and its corrals.

The position of the butts of the horizontal poles and presence of the post-molds suggest that they once stood vertically to serve as a manger. Unfortunately no organic matter on the floor in the unpaved section was saved but the description fits a soft yellow-green material which at Pueblo de las Humanas was identified definitely as rotted corn stover. The paved area would provide drainage for overnight stabling of work oxen. The gate leading to the fields rather than to the corral also suggests draft animals.

One more corral was added when a long narrow enclosure, 19 by 145 feet, was abutted to the south wall of area B to run parallel to the south wall of area G. Nothing remains but low masonry footing. If a west wall ever existed it was removed when the State of New Mexico built a small contact station for visitors over the spot. Except that it was built after all the other large enclosures described, nothing can be said about the time it was used. Though it may have pertained to the late mission period, it may have been built after mission and pueblo were abandoned.

Domínguez' description of the church has been compared with features that can still be identified today. Now let us follow him through the convento and attempt to reconcile what he saw with the foregoing interpretation of the remains. Quotations are directly from the Adams and Chávez translation.

> As we enter the church, on our right under the choir is the entrance to an old church outside the wall. The old building extends to the south, with the door where I said, and is joined to the convent on the Epistle side. And in order not to become involved, I state now that it is of a size to fit into the nave of the one we are describing and that it is falling down. As we enter the old church, outside its wall on the left is the sacristy now in use, and the baptistery now in use is on the right, also outside the walls, and the entrance to both rooms is from the old building.

Fray Francisco has gone through the door in the south nave wall into area I, Zeinos' "chapel," the memory of which would easily survive the seventy years since it was abandoned. The building does not "extend" to the south but it lies to the south and extends east. But this discrepancy is a matter of semantics. The sacristy *is* to the left of this long room. The door to what I have identified as the baptistry is somewhat to the right but is also in front of him through the south wall of the old church. The small door in the wall to his right leads to what he, later, and all other evidence, identifies as the porter's lodge. Since the convento joined the Epistle side we know the orientation was the same as the later church—with the sanctuary to the east.

. . . with regard to the baptistery, I state that it is a small room with a window, a door, a small pillar and an earthen bowl like those I have described elsewhere.

We have now gone through the door in the southwest corner of area I into a room nine feet square built into the northwest corner of the cloister. Walls, upon excavation, were too low to reveal a window but it must have looked out on either the west or the north ambulatory.

At this point Domínguez backtracks to resume his description of the church and cemetery. Later he returns to the convento.

The porter's lodge is inside the cemetery facing north, and it is a square portico measuring 10 varas divided equally. There is a strong cross timber in the center of the roof, and two wooden pillars at the mouth, which divide it into three arches, with railings in the ones at the sides. There are adobe seats around it and an ordinary two-leaved door with a crossbar in the middle of the center wall.

There can be no doubt about the placement of the porter's lodge as shown in Fig. 5, but there are other minor discrepancies. Domínguez' *vara* can be computed at 33 inches from the measurements given for the church which could be checked. This would make the lodge 27.5 feet square. Witkind mapped it as 20 feet long against the north wall of the convento but described it in his notes as 25 feet. He found no north wall but, anticipating publication of the 1776 account, postulated an open portal. Pinkley describes the door in the middle of the south wall as a white-plastered niche 3.1 feet deep by 4.2 feet wide with its sill about a foot above the floor and opening into room 14, and restored it as such. Witkind described it as a door, with reveal splayed to the south, and partly plugged with adobes.

As we enter the aforesaid [the door in the porter's lodge], there are two beautiful stables, each with a strawloft, on our right. One is on a corner, and around the corner is a stair well with stairs leading to the upper story, which we shall soon see.

The friar has entered rooms 14-15 which are now one again after removal of the partitions. Rooms 52 and 53 are evidently his stables. Room 53 is "on a corner" and if one went out a door that no longer exists in the west wall he would have to go "around the corner" to reach the stairwell, room 50 with its half-floor on the second story.

> Beyond the stairwell is a cell, then a passageway which I shall describe later . . .

The cell would be room 48 with its corner fireplace. The door in the south wall leads to the "passageway," room 46. Rather than come back to it later, let us pull forward his postponed lines relating to it.

> The passageway I left pending further mention leads to a fortified tower which stands on one side of the convent. When there are enemies, a stone mortar is installed in it.

With its massive walls and floor four to five feet above the plain, room 45 was in a good position to command approaches to the church, convento, and corrals. Returning now to his first mention of the passage, Domínguez says:

> . . . then another cell on the corner. There are six rooms around the corner as far as the inside corner against the old building, and of all these six, only one, which serves as a fine storeroom, has a door, but no key.

Room 17 is in the southwest corner of the cloister and beyond it are six rooms—13, 12, 11, 10, 9 and 8. Room 8, the only room in the convento with a wooden sill, would be the storeroom.

> On the left as we enter, [he is back at the starting point in room 14 just inside the porter's lodge] the wall of the baptistery extends to the inside corner of the old building to that inside corner where the six rooms are. In this corner, and in the cloister itself, is another stairway, which leads to the upper story like the one mentioned above.

He is describing the east wall of room 14 abutting the north wall of the convento which is followed east to the stairway next to room 8. Room 7 was no more than a small closet or cupboard under the stairs.

The rest of the 1776 account deals with features which had disappeared long before the earliest excavation.

> Whichever of the afore-mentioned stairways we ascend, we see rooms over the lower ones mentioned, but I note that those over the porter's lodge are in bad condition, as are those

around the corner to the west. Only those that face south and are approached by the stairway in the corner of the cloister are usable. In these south rooms and in the ones on the west there are very good miradores, one on each side. The south one has a good railing. The other is bare because, according to what the Indians say, an alcalde who was here (and he still lives here but is no longer alcalde), called Vicente Armijo, took the balusters to put them in the *casas reales*. The upper cloister is open, with railing between wooden pillars.

The *miradores* were probably small, balconied windows looking out to the south and west. The reference to the *casas reales*, the government buildings, and to the resident Spaniard is particularly interesting.

In the summer of 1970 two outlying structures of apparent Spanish construction were tested. They lay near the convento but were not an integral part of the mission complex. The largest of these, 240 feet west of area A and midway between the convento and the banks of Arroyo del Pueblo, was a compound measuring 305 feet north-south and 126 feet east-west (Fig. 16). The central area was an open yard with inside measurements of roughly 120 by 140 feet. Appended to the north and south sides were smaller pens or corrals. Along the east side of one of the smaller pens at the north end of the complex was a series of rooms. Two of these were excavated (Fig. 17). They were about 8 feet square with low stone walls from 1.5 to 3.0 feet thick. Masonry was a maximum of 2 feet high and the loose stone in the fill was not plentiful enough to have raised them much higher. The upper walls were probably of adobe but none survived. The rooms were featureless except for a drain-opening 1.4 feet wide and half as high at the base of one wall. The rusted steel blade of a clasp knife was found in the vent. A steel arrowhead and a copper button were found in other trenches in the compound.

We know that Governor Vélez sent a garrison of soldiers to Pecos in 1750 and that they were still there in late 1751 when they helped the Pecos warriors throw back a strong Comanche force. If the garrison was meant to be permanent they would have probably constructed a presidio including barracks, stables, and fortifications. This may be the location of the "mouth of the trench where the squad was" described by Vélez. The outlines are not incompatible with plans of other Spanish presidios of the eighteenth century.[17]

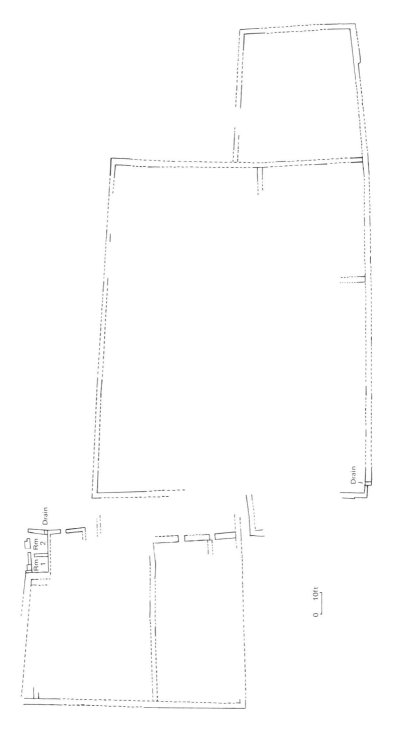

16. Plan of presidio.

Drain

Rm 1 Rm 2 Drain

0 10ft

17.   Rooms 1 and 2, presidio. (National Park Service photograph)

The second of the outlying features is a string of contiguous rooms 60 and 70 feet west of the convento approximately halfway from the latter to the large compound. The house was 145 feet long by about 30 to 40 feet wide. It ran south from a point opposite the north end of the stable (rooms 40-42) to another 70 feet west of area A's southwest corner. It was tested in three places. The north end was trenched outside a stone footing 2.5 feet wide through a foot or more of rich trash containing much animal bone. One room 9 feet square at the south end was excavated (Fig. 18). Stone foundations were up to 3 feet wide and a wide fireplace was built into the middle of the east wall. There was no trace of a superstructure but underlying walls indicate that there was rebuilding here at least two times. A small Sikyatki Polychrome bowl lay on the floor.

Two rooms were excavated near the center of the house. These, like the one described above, were dwellings. One, measuring 8 by 12 feet, was floored with adobe brick in a herring-bone pattern and had a small fireplace of grass-tempered adobes in one corner. A plain culinary jar sat in the ashes of the fireplace and a small polished red bowl on the floor. This room had been partly excavated earlier—probably by Kidder as it shows on Lindbergh's 1929 aerial photograph.

Adjacent to it was another room of the same size with a cobblestone floor (Fig. 19). Against a shorter wall was a bench 2 feet deep of earth faced with standing stone slabs. The slabs rose 0.4 foot above the flagged surface which was covered with a thick deposit of ashes containing burned animal bone. Though the bench stood only 0.8 foot above the floor, it seemed to be a cooking area similar to that in room 24 in the convento. Except for the low elevation of the bench it resembles a common Spanish colonial stove which was usually equipped with a hood and stood about 30 inches above the floor. Also suggestive of a kitchen was a subfloor drain which crossed the room. The ditch was 1.0 foot deep by 0.8 foot wide and lined with standing slabs of stone. Small sticks laid across the top on 0.3 to 0.4 foot centers supported a flagstone covering. The ditch entered through the north wall and went out under the south. A piece of fired brick in the fill suggests the wall construction and a cut fragment of split selenite may have been from a window. The only artifacts in the room were a chipped end-scraper of Alibates flint, a crudely-cut brass pendant, and a mano. Pieces of candlesticks of red polished pottery were found in both rooms.

18.   Room 3, *Casas Reales*. (National Park Service photograph)

19.   Room 1, *Casas Reales*.

Sherds from all three investigated areas of the house and compound included Tewa Polychrome, Kotyití Glaze-polychrome, Majolica, Chinese porcelain, and wheel-turned olive jars with green-glazed interiors.

It is tempting to speculate that this building was the *casas reales* that received the balusters taken from the convento. We know there was a garrison stationed at Pecos intermittently through the 1750s and '60s and it is logical to assume that wives and families accompanied it since that was the usual pattern. Domínguez mentions two Spaniards living at the pueblo—the current alcalde, Don José Herrera, and the ex-alcalde, Vicente Armijo. There may well have been others and these two structures probably represent the beginning of a secular Spanish presence that continues in the modern community of Pecos. Both features would bear more investigation, as would a large stone corral to the west across the arroyo and a stone quadrangle below the west edge of the mesilla.

Although a priest, first from Santa Fe and later from San Miguel, continued to minister to the eroding population of the pueblo, the convento ceased to be important to the mission after 1792 when it was officially declared a *visita* without a resident minister. It had been deteriorating, both in importance and materially, for twenty years. But it is obvious that some use was made of the rooms and corrals even after abandonment of the pueblo. Witkind found heavy manure deposits above the floors of area I, the cloister, and rooms 3 and 14—evidence of their use as sheepfolds or pens for other stock by local settlers or overnight campers on the Santa Fe trail. Several additions to the architecture probably relate to those activities. These include small jacales built on an accumulation of manure in the northwest and northeast corners of area G, five small rooms built on fill in area D, and two more in area C.

One final addition was apparently made while there was an effort to maintain the convento for some purpose or another. A wall of red adobes on a shallow stone footing was run from the southeast corner of room 46, roughly parallel to the south walls of rooms 18 through 21, to join the common south corner of rooms 21 and 22. The bottom of the foundation was at a somewhat higher level than the walls of the earlier rooms. The long corridor which was created tapered from 3 feet wide between rooms 46 and 18 down to 1 foot at the east end, and the space was filled with earth. Its purpose seems to have been that of a curtain wall to provide extra support to this row of rooms, which was originally intended to be no more than one story when built in the 1620s but it supported a second story after the post-revolt rebuilding. Subsequently rectangular buttresses 7.5 feet square were added at each end of the curtain wall to add still more support. Earth-cored masonry walls 1.6 and 3.0 feet high are all that remains and if adobe buttressing rose above them all traces have disappeared. The foot of the masonry lies several inches above level of the base of the curtain wall foundation, evidence that they were later additions. A Spanish *real* (Fig. 20) bearing the date 1784 was found in the mortar between the stones of one of the buttresses but I suspect it found its way there considerably after that date.

Certainly one of the last bits of construction at the Pecos convento was a tower with an oval outline lying across the east wall of area E (Fig. 21). That part of the tower lying within the courtyard sat on up to 3.1 feet of alluvial and wind-blown soil that had banked against the inside of the east wall to reach the top of what remained standing. Outside the court there was no build-up of fill and the tower's base stood very near the original ground level. At the time of excavation the tower's walls stood from 0.9 to 3.2 feet high. An unprepared floor level just above the top of the convento's outer wall was covered with "3-4 inches of charcoal and ash and bright red burned adobe." Presumably the burned adobe was from a roof. Remaining stone masonry was probably the foundation of an adobe structure as there was little loose stone in the vicinity.

Gregorio Ruiz of Pecos, born in the 1880s, remembers that the tower stood an estimated fifteen feet high when he was a child, and was pierced with loopholes. His grandfather told him that as a young man he used to take his turn at standing guard here against attacks of the Ollero Apaches. This was presumably in the first half of the nineteenth century.

The church and convento of Nuestra Señora de los Angeles de Porciúncula have now been pretty well exploited archaeologically but there remain other areas which can still add to the story of Spanish occupation of the mesilla of Pecos. The presidio and the *casas reales* were only tested and there has been no digging in a system of reservoirs and what appears to be a walled garden between the mission and the arroyo to the northwest. Excavation of the large corral across the arroyo may reveal something about the Comanchero trade of the eighteenth century, and work at the southern end of the south pueblo should uncover temporary

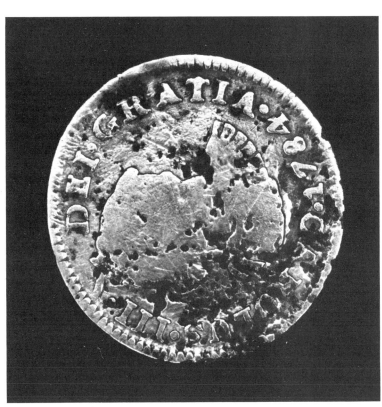

20. A Spanish *real* from a buttress in area H. (National Park Service photograph)

21. Tower in area E. (National Park Service photograph)

quarters used by Fray Andrés Suárez while his new church was under construction. But perhaps the archivist digging through musty files of the Council of the Indies in Seville can shed more light than an archaeologist troweling the red clay of Pecos. The Spanish bureaucrat of three hundred years ago was no less the compulsive copyist than his modern counterpart, and buried in the vaults there must be much fascinating detail of his greed and sacrifice, his dedication and boredom, and the long struggle for survival in New Mexico.

22. Pecos mission: the pueblo is on the ridge to the left and the ruts of the Santa Fe Trail are visible on the right. (Koogle and Pouls photograph)

23. Pecos mission with the ruins of the pueblo behind it. (National Park Service photograph)

24. The church before excavation. (National Park Service photograph)

25. Stabilized foundation on the 17th century. (National Park Service photograph)

26. Glorieta Mesa from the stabilized nave. (National Park Service photograph)

27. A reconstructed kiva, Pecos Pueblo. (National Park Service photograph)

28. View south to Glorieta Mesa across the south pueblo. (National Park Service photograph)

29. Rosary beads from the convento. (National Park Service photograph)

Notes

Introduction

1. Adolph F. Bandelier, "A Visit to the Aboriginal Ruins of the Valley of the Rio Pecos," Papers of the Archaeological Institute of America (Boston, 1881), p. 34–133; Charles H. Lange and Carroll L. Riley, *The Southwestern Journals of Adolph F. Bandelier, 1880–1882* (Albuquerque: University of New Mexico Press, 1966), pp. 74–83.

2. Alfred V. Kidder, "Pecos, New Mexico: Archaeological Notes," Papers of the Robert S. Peabody Foundation for Archaeology (Andover, Mass., 1958), p. 329.

3. Edgar L. Hewett and Reginald G. Fisher, *Mission Monuments of New Mexico* (Albuquerque: University of New Mexico Press, 1943), p. 204.

4. Stanley A. Stubbs, Bruce T. Ellis, and Alfred E. Dittert, "The 'Lost' Pecos Church," *El Palacio* 64, pts. 3–4 (Santa Fe, N.M., 1957): 67–92.

PART I
Historical Background

1. George P. Hammond and Agapito Rey, *Narratives of the Coronado Expedition* (Albuquerque: University of New Mexico Press, 1940), vol. 2, p. 270; Adolph F. Bandelier, "Documentary History of the Rio Grande Pueblos," *New Mexico Historical Review* 5 (hereafter referred to as *NMHR*) (1930): 176.

2. France V. Scholes and Lansing B. Bloom, "Friar Personnel and Mission Chronology," *NMHR* 19 (1944): 328.

3. Angélico Chávez, *Coronado's Friars*, Academy of American Franciscan History, Monograph Series, vol. 8 (Washington, D.C., 1968), pp. 41–42.

4. Scholes and Bloom, "Friar Personnel," p. 323.

5. Ibid., vol. 20 (1945): 67.

6. France V. Scholes, "Church and State in New Mexico, 1610–1650," *NMHR* 11 (1936): 169.

7. Frederick W. Hodge, George P. Hammond, and Agapito Rey, *Fray Alonso de Benavides' Revised Memorial of 1634*, Coronado Historical Series, vol. 4 (Albuquerque: University of New Mexico Press, 1945), p. 67.

8. Nels C. Nelson, "Chronology of the Tano Ruins," American Museum of Natural History, Anthropological Papers, vol. 15, pt. 1 (New York, 1916), p. 98.

9. Lansing B. Bloom, "Fray Estevan de Perea's *Relación*," *NMHR* 8, no. 1 (1933): 228.

10. Alden C. Hayes, "The Missing Convento of San Isidro," *El Palacio* 75, no. 4 (Santa Fe, N.M., 1968): 35–40.

11. Stubbs, Ellis, and Dittert, "The 'Lost' Pecos Church," p. 85.

12. Stanley A. Stubbs, " 'New' Old Churches Found at Quarai and Tabira," *El Palacio* 66, no. 5 (Santa Fe, N.M., 1959): 162–69.

13. Agustín de Vetancourt, *Crónica de la Provincia de Santa Evangelio de México* (Mexico, D.F.: Biblioteca de la Iberia, 1871), p. 323.

14. Eleanor B. Adams and Angélico Chávez, *The Missions of New Mexico, 1776* (Albuquerque: University of New Mexico Press, 1956), p. 208–14.

15. George Kubler, *The Religious Architecture of New Mexico*, 4th ed. (Colorado Springs, Colo.: The Taylor Museum, 1940; reprint ed., Albuquerque: University of New Mexico Press, 1972), p. 18.

16. Scholes and Bloom, "Friar Personnel," p. 66.

17. France V. Scholes, "Documents for the History of New Mexico Missions in the 17th Century," *NMHR* 4 (1929): 47–48.

18. Ibid., p. 46.

19. France V. Scholes, "Correction to 'Documents,' " *NMHR* 19 (1944): 245.

20. Scholes, "Church and State," p. 300.

21. Ibid., p. 42.

22. France V. Scholes, "Troublous Times in New Mexico, 1659–1670," *NMHR* 16 (1941): 50.

23. Ralph E. Twitchell, *The Spanish Archives of New Mexico*, vol. 2 (Cedar Rapids: Torch Press, 1914), p. 17; Charles W. Hackett and Charmion C. Shelby, *The Revolt of the Pueblo Indians of New Mexico and Otermin's Attempted Reconquest*, Coronado Historical Series, vol. 8 (Albuquerque: University of New Mexico Press, 1942), p. 11.

24. Charles W. Hackett, *Historical Documents Relating to New Mexico, Nueva Vizcaya, and Approaches Thereto, to 1773*, vol. 3 (Washington, D.C.: Carnegie Institution, 1937), p. 336.

25. Ibid., p. 336.

26. France V. Scholes, "The Supply Service of the New Mexico Missions in the 17th Century," *NMHR* 5 (1930): 210.

27. Lansing B. Bloom and Lynn B. Mitchell, "The Chapter Elections in 1672," *NMHR* 13 (1938): 114.

28. Twitchell, *Spanish Archives*, p. 57.

29. Hackett and Shelby, *Revolt*, p. liii.

30. Vetancourt, *Crónica*, p. 323.

31. Irving A. Leonard, *The Mercurio Volante of Don Carlos Siguenza y Góngora*, no. 3 (Los Angeles: Quivira Society Publications, 1932), p. 74.

32. José M. Espinosa, *Crusaders of the Rio Grande: The Story of Don Diego de Vargas and the Reconquest and Refounding of New Mexico* (Chicago: Institute of Jesuit History, 1942), p. 158.

33. Jessie B. Bailey, *Diego de Vargas and the Reconquest of New Mexico* (Albuquerque: University of New Mexico Press, 1940), p. 176.

34. Ibid.

35. Espinosa, *Crusaders*, p. 243.

36. Ralph E. Twitchell, "The Pueblo Revolt of 1696," *Old Santa Fe* 3 (1916): 356.

37. Espinosa, *Crusaders*, p. 350.

38. Audiencia de Guadalajara, legajo 141.

39. Adams and Chávez, *Missions*, p. 332; Fray Angélico Chávez, *Archives of the Archdiocese of Santa Fe*, Academy of American Franciscan History (Washington, D.C., 1957), pp. 249–57.

40. Hackett, *Historical Documents*, p. 373.

41. Twitchell, *Spanish Archives*, p. 133.

42. Oakah L. Jones, *Pueblo Warrior and Spanish Conquest* (Norman: University of Oklahoma Press, 1966), p. 91.

43. Ibid.

44. Albert H. Schroeder, "A Study of the Apache Indians. Part III, The Mescalero Apaches," mimeographed (U.S. Department of Justice, Washington, D.C., 1960).

45. Jones, *Pueblo Warrior*, p. 96.

46. Lansing B. Bloom, "A Campaign against the Moqui Pueblos under Governor Phelix Martínez," *NMHR* 6 (1931): 175–86.

47. Jones, *Pueblo Warrior*, p. 97.

48. Ibid.

49. A. B. Thomas, *The Plains Indians and New Mexico*, Coronado Historical Series, vol. 11 (Albuquerque: University of New Mexico Press, 1940), p. 17.

50. Henry W. Kelly, "The Franciscan Missions of New Mexico, 1740–1760," *NMHR* 16 (1941): 82.

51. My translation from José A. Villa-Señor y Sánchez, *Teatro americano, descripción general de los reynos y provincias de la Nueva España*, pt. 2 (Madrid: Impresora viuda Hogal, 1748), p. 413.

52. Kelly, "The Franciscan Missions," pp. 89–90.

53. Chávez, *Archives*, p. 234.

54. Ibid., p. 31.

55. Thomas, *The Plains Indians*, p. 20.

56. Ibid., p. 25.

57. Ibid., p. 68.

58. Jones, *Pueblo Warrior*, p. 137.

59. Ibid.

60. Thomas, *The Plains Indians*, p. 45.

61. Chávez, *Archives*, p. 234.

62. Adams and Chávez, *Missions*, p. 214.

63. Ibid., p. 212.

64. Chávez, *Archives*, pp. 245–55.

65. Adams and Chávez, *Missions*, p. 213.

66. Chávez, *Archives*, p. 253.

67. Hodge, Hammond, and Rey, *Fray Alonso*, p. 273.

68. Chávez, *Archives*, p. 75.

69. Ibid., p. 77.

70. Ibid., p. 205.

71. Ibid., p. 244.

72. John P. Harrington, "The Ethnogeography of the Tewa Indians," Bureau of American Ethnology, 29th Annual Report (Washington, D.C., 1916), p. 477.

73. Elsie C. Parsons, *The Pueblo of Jemez* (New Haven: Yale University Press, 1925), p. 133.

74. Ibid., genealogical tables, end pocket.

PART II
Architectural Sequence

1. Stubbs, Ellis, and Dittert, "The 'Lost' Pecos Church," p. 75.

2. Kidder, "Pecos, New Mexico," p. 191.

3. Vetancourt, *Crónica*, p. 323.

4. Gordon Vivian, *Excavations in a 17th Century Jumano Pueblo, Gran Quivira*, National Park Service Archeological Research Series, no. 8 (Washington, D.C., 1964), p. 86.

5. Watson Smith, Richard B. Woodbury, and Nathalie F. Woodbury, "The Excavation of Hawikuh by Frederick Webb Hodge," Contributions from the Museum of the American Indian Heye Foundation, vol. 20 (New York, 1966), p. 118.

6. Ross G. Montgomery, Watson Smith, and J. O. Brew, "Franciscan Awatovi," Papers of the Peabody Museum of Archaeology and Ethnology (Cambridge, Mass., 1949), p. 8.

7. Kidder, "Pecos, New Mexico," p. 236.

8. Alden C. Hayes, "The Excavation of Mound 7, Gran Quivira," manuscript (Washington, D.C., Office of Archeology, 1970), pp. 188–89.

9. Hackett and Shelby, *Revolt*, pp. 207, 225.

10. Montgomery, Smith, and Brew, "Franciscan Awatovi," p. 65.

11. Joseph H. Toulouse, *The Mission of San Gregorio de Abo*, Monographs of the School of American Research, no. 13 (Albuquerque: University of New Mexico Press, 1949), p. 11.

12. "Kivas Found at Quarai Monastery," *El Palacio* 40, nos. 22–24 (Santa Fe, N.M., 1957): 122.

13. Montgomery, Smith, and Brew, "Franciscan Awatovi," p. 48; Smith, Woodbury and Woodbury, "Hawikuh," p. 121.

14. William H. Emory, Notes of a Military Reconnaissance . . . , to the 30th Congress, 1st session, 1848, Senate Executive Document no. 7, Washington, D.C.

15. Adams and Chávez, *Missions*, pp. 208–14.

16. Kubler, *Religious Architecture*, p. 38.

17. Rex E. Gerald, "Spanish Presidios of the Late 18th Century in Northern New Spain," Museum of New Mexico Research Records (Santa Fe, 1968).

Bibliography

Adams, Eleanor B., and Chávez, Angélico. *The Missions of New Mexico, 1776.* Albuquerque: University of New Mexico Press, 1956.

Audiencia de Guadalajara, legajo 141. n.d.

Bailey, Jessie B. *Diego de Vargas and the Reconquest of New Mexico.* Albuquerque: University of New Mexico Press, 1940.

Bandelier, Adolph F. "A Visit to the Aboriginal Ruins of the Valley of the Rio Pecos." Papers of the Archaeological Institute of America, vol. 1, no. 2. Boston, 1881.

———. "Documentary History of the Rio Grande Pueblos, New Mexico." *New Mexico Historical Review* 5 (1930): 176.

Bloom, Lansing B. "A Campaign against the Moqui Pueblos under Governor Phelix Martinez." *New Mexico Historical Review* 6 (1931):

———. "Fray Estevan de Perea's Relación." *New Mexico Historical Review* 8 (1933): 228.

——— and Mitchell, Lynn B. "The Chapter Elections in 1672." *New Mexico Historical Review* 13 (1938): 114.

Chávez, Angélico. *Archives of the Archdiocese of Santa Fe.* Academy of American Franciscan History. Washington, D.C., 1957.

———. *Coronado's Friars.* Academy of American Franciscan History, Monograph Series, vol. 8. Washington, D.C., 1968.

Emory, William H. Notes of a Military Reconnaissance. . . . 30th Congress 1st session. Senate Executive Document, no. 7. Washington, D.C., 1848.

Espinosa, José M. *Crusaders of the Rio Grande: The Story of Don Diego de Vargas and the Reconquest and Refounding of New Mexico.* Chicago: Institute of Jesuit History, 1942.

Gerald, Rex E. "Spanish Presidios of the Late 18th Century in Northern New Spain." Museum of New Mexico Research Records, no. 7. Santa Fe, 1968.

Hackett, Charles W. *Historical Documents Relating to New Mexico, Nueva Vizcaya, and Approaches Thereto, to 1773.* Vol. 3. Washington, D.C.: Carnegie Institution, 1937.

——— and Shelby, Charmion C. *The Revolt of the Pueblo Indians of New Mexico and Otermin's Attempted Reconquest.* Coronado Historical Series, vols. 8–9. Albuquerque: University of New Mexico Press, 1942.

Hammond, George P. and Rey, Agapito. *Narratives of the Coronado Expedition.* Coronado Historical Series, vol. 2. Albuquerque: University of New Mexico Press, 1940.

Harrington, John P. "The Ethnogeography of the Tewa Indians." Bureau of American Ethnology, 29th Annual Report (Washington, D.C., 1916): 477.

Hayes, Alden C. "The Missing Convento of San Isidro." El Palacio 75 (1968): 35–40.

———. "The Excavation of Mound 7, Gran Quivira." Manuscript, New Mexico Archeological Center (Albuquerque, 1970): 188–89.

Hewett, Edgar L. and Fisher, Reginald G. Mission Monuments of New Mexico. Albuquerque: University of New Mexico Press, 1943.

Hodge, Frederick W., Hammond, George P., and Rey, Agapito. Fray Alonso de Benavides' Revised Memorial of 1634. Coronado Historical Series, vol. 4. Albuquerque: University of New Mexico Press. 1945.

Jones, Oakah L. Pueblo Warrior and Spanish Conquest. Norman: University of Oklahoma Press, 1966.

Kelly, Henry W. "The Franciscan Missions of New Mexico, 1740–1760." New Mexico Historical Review 16 (1941): 82.

Kidder, Alfred V. "Pecos, New Mexico: Archaeological Notes." Papers of the Robert S. Peabody Foundation for Archaeology (Andover, Mass., 1958): 329.

"Kivas Found at Quarai Monastery." El Palacio 40 (1936): 122.

Kubler, George. The Religious Architecture of New Mexico. The Taylor Museum, 1940; reprint ed., Albuquerque: University of New Mexico Press, 1972.

Lange, Charles H. and Riley, Carroll L. The Southwestern Journals of Adolph F. Bandelier, 1880–1882. Albuquerque: University of New Mexico Press, 1966.

Leonard, Irving A. The Mercurio Volante of Don Carlos Siguenza y Góngora. Los Angeles: Quivira Society Publications, no. 3, 1932.

Montgomery, Ross G., Smith, Watson, and Brew, J. O. "Franciscan Awatovi." Papers of the Peabody Museum of Archaeology and Ethnology (Cambridge, Mass., 1949): 8.

Nelson, Nels C. "Chronology of the Tano Ruins." American Museum of Natural History, Anthropological Papers, vol. 15, part 1 (New York, 1916): 98.

Parsons, Elsie C. The Pueblo of Jemez. New Haven: Yale University Press, 1925.

Scholes, France V. "Documents for the History of New Mexico Missions in the 17th Century." New Mexico Historical Review 4 (1929): 47–48.

———. "The Supply Service of the New Mexico Missions in the 17th Century." New Mexico Historical Review 5 (1930): 210.

———. "Church and State in New Mexico, 1610–1650." New Mexico Historical Review 11 and 12 (1936–37): 169.

———. "Troublous Times in New Mexico, 1659–1670." New Mexico Historical Review 16 (1941): 50.

———. "Correction. (Documents for the History of New Mexico in the 17th Century)." New Mexico Historical Review 19 (1944): 245.

——— and Bloom, Lansing B. "Friar Personnel and Mission Chronology." New Mexico Historical Review 19 and 20 (1944–45): 328.

Schroeder, Albert H. "A Study of the Apache Indians." Part III, The Mescalero Apaches. Mimeographed (U.S. Department of Justice, Washington, D.C., 1960).

Smith, Watson, Woodbury, Richard B., and Woodbury, Nathalie F. "The Excavation of Hawikuh by Frederick Webb Hodge." Contributions from the Museum of the American Indian Heye Foundation, vol. 20 (New York, 1966): 118.

Stubbs, Stanley A. " 'New' Old Churches Found at Quarai and Tabira." *El Palacio* 66 (1959): 162–69.

———, Ellis, Bruce T. and Dittert, Alfred E. "The 'Lost' Pecos Church." *El Palacio* 64, nos. 3–4 (1957): 67–92.

Thomas, A. B. *The Plains Indians and New Mexico.* Coronado Historical Series, vol. 11. Albuquerque: University of New Mexico Press, 1940.

Toulouse, Joseph H. *The Mission of San Gregorio de Abo.* Monographs of the School of American Research, no. 13. Albuquerque: University of New Mexico Press, 1949.

Twitchell, Ralph E. *The Spanish Archives of New Mexico.* 2 vols. Cedar Rapids, Iowa: Torch Press, 1914.

———. "The Pueblo Revolt of 1696." *Old Santa Fe* 3 (Santa Fe, 1916): 356.

Vetancurt, Agustín de. *Crónica de la Provincia de Santa Evangelio de México.* Mexico: Biblioteca de la Iberia, 1871.

Villa-Señor y Sánchez, José A. *Teatro Americano, Descripción General de los Reynos y Provincias de la Nueva España.* Pt. 2. Madrid: Impresora viuda Hogal, 1748.

Vivian, Gordon. *Excavations in a 17th Century Jumano Pueblo, Gran Quivira.* National Park Service Archeological Research Series, no. 8. Washington, D.C., 1964.

Index

Abó, San Gregorio de, 32
Abó Pueblo, 32
Adams, Eleanor B., xiii, 50, 68, 69, 70, 71
Alameda, 8
Alpuente, Juan, 9, 10
Alvarez, Juan, 11
Anton Chico, 13
Apache Indians, xi, 6, 11, 12-14
  see also Indian conflicts
Archeological Institute of America, xii
Armijo, Vicente, 58
Arranegui, José de, 11-12, 24, 35, 42
Awatovi, 32, 35

Bailey, Jessie B., 68, 71
Bandelier, Adolph F., xi-xii, 35, 67, 71
Benavides, Alonso de, 3, 4-5
Bera, Domingo de, 7
Bernalillo, 10
Bloom, Lansing B., 67, 68, 69, 71
Brew, J. O., 70, 72

Caballeros, Juan de los, 2
Cachupín, Tomás Vélez, 14-15
Castaño, 1-2
Chapman, Kenneth, xii
Chávez, Angélico, xiii, 50, 67, 68, 69, 70, 71
Cicuye, xi
Cochití, 10
Codallos, 13, 14, 15
Comanche Indians, xi, 12, 13, 14-15, 16, 17
  see also Indian conflicts
Corbera, Francisco, 8, 10
Corbett, John, 35
Coronado, Francisco Vázquez de, xi, 1
Cunixi, 10

Dios, Juan de, 2
Dittert, Alfred, xiii, 67, 68, 70, 73
Domínguez, Francisco Atanasio, xiii, 4,
16-17, 35, 37, 40, 41-42, 43, 45, 46, 50-53, 58

El Paso, 8, 9
Ellis, Bruce T., xiii, 67, 68, 70, 73
Emory, William H., 37, 70, 71
Espejo, Antonio de, 1, 2
Espinosa, José M., 68, 71
Eulate, Juan de, 3

Felipe, Don, 10, 12, 13
Ferdon, Edwin N., xiii
Fisher, Reginald G., 67, 72

Galisteo, 2, 7, 13, 14, 15
Gerald, Rex E., 70, 71
Gerónimo, Don, 13
Glorieta Mesa, 35
Guadalajara, Audiencia de, 68
Guerrero, José Cristóbal, 17

Hackett, Charles W., 68, 69, 70, 71
Hammond, George P., 67, 69, 71, 72
Harrington, John P., 69, 72
Hawikuh, 3, 35
Hayes, Alden C., 67, 70, 72
Herrera, Don José, 58
Hewett, Edgar L., xii, xiii, 67, 72
Hodge, Frederick W., 67, 69, 72
Hopi Indians, 13

Indian conflicts, xi, 7-11, 12-16, 32
Isleta, 6, 8, 41

Jémez, 10, 18
Jesús, Domingo de, 9
Jones, Oakah L., 69, 72

Kelly, Henry W., 69, 72
Kidder, A. V., xii, xiii, 32, 35, 56, 67, 70, 72
Kivas, 32-35, 48
Kubler, George, 68, 70, 72

La Purísima Concepción de Aguicu, 25
Ladron Mountains, 13
Lange, Charles H., 67, 72
Lentz, Robert, 3
Leonard, Irving A., 68, 72
Lindbergh, Charles A., xiii, 56
Llano Estacado, 13

McKusick, Charmion R., 34
Manzano Mountains, 2
Marín, José García, 10
Matlock, Gary, 33-34
Mandinueta, 16
Missions of New Mexico, 1776, The (Adams), xiii
Mitchell, Lynn B., 68, 71
Mogollón, Flores, 12
Montgomery, Ross G., 70, 72
Museum of New Mexico, ix, xii, xiii

Nambé, 5
National Park Service, ix, xiii
Nelson, Nels C., 67, 72
Nuestra Señora de Guadalupe, 8
Nuestra Señora de la Concepción, 32
Nuestra Señora de los Angeles, 3-4
Nuestra Señora de Porciúncula, 11-12
Nuestra Señora de Porciúncula de los Angeles, 17
Nusbaum, Jesse L., xii, xiv, 41

Oñate, Juan de, xi, 2
Oraibi, 6
Ortega, Pedro de, 2, 3, 5
Otermín, Antonio de, 7, 8, 32

Pajarito Plateau, xii
Palacio, José, 17
Parsons, Elsie C., 69, 72
Pecos National Monument, ix, xiv
Pecos River, 13, 16, 17
Pedrosa, Juan de, 7
Peinado, Alonso de, 2
Peñalosa Briceño y Berdugo, Dionisio de, 7
Peralta, Pedro de, 6
Perea, Estevan de, 6
Phillips Academy Expedition, xii
Picurís, 10, 12-13
Pinkley, Jean M., ix, xiii, xiv, 3, 5, 20, 22, 30, 35, 48, 51
Piro Indians, 8
Pojoaque, 41

Posada, Alonso de, 7
Puaray, 8
Pueblo de las Humanas, 32, 49
Pueblo Indians, 15

Quarai, 4, 32
Queres Indians, 8

Rey, Agapito, 67, 69, 71, 72
Richert, Roland S., xiv
Riley, Carroll L., 67, 72
Rio Grande, 2
Rosas, Luis de, 6
Ruiz, Gregorio, 59

Salinas Province, 2, 4
San Antonio de Padua, 18, 40
San Bernardo, 32
San Buenaventura de las Humanas, 25
San Diego de Jémez, 18
San Estevan de Acoma, 5
San Felipe, 10
San Gabriel del Yunque, 2
San Ildefonso, 2, 10, 41
San Isidro de las Humanas, 3
San Jose de Jémez, 5
San Juan, 2, 41
San Lázaro, 3
San Marcos, 7, 8
San Miguel, 17, 58
San Miguel, Francisco de, 2
Sandía, 5, 6, 8, 18, 32
Sandía Mountains, 2, 12
Santa Cruz, 10
Santa Fe, 4, 7, 8, 9, 10, 16, 17, 58
Santa Fe Trail, xi, xii
Santo Domingo, 10
Scholes, France V., 5, 67, 68, 72
Schroeder, Albert H., ix, 69, 72
Senecú, 5
Sesafweyah (Agustín Pecos), 18
Sevilleta, 32
Shelby, Charmion C., 68, 70, 71
Smith, Watson, 70, 72
Socorro, 8
Stanley, John Mix, 37
Stubbs, Stanley A., xiii, 67, 68, 70, 73
Suárez, Andrés, 3, 4-5, 19-20, 28, 61

Tabirá, 4, 6
Taos, 2, 6, 10, 12, 13, 14
Tesuque, 7
Thomas, A. B., 69, 73

Tinoco, Manuel de, 7
Toulouse, Joseph H., 70, 73
Trizio, Miguel de, 10
Twitchell, Ralph E., 68, 69, 73

Ubeda, Luis de, 1
Ute Indians, 12

Valliant, Susanna B., xii, xiv
Vargas, Diego de, 8, 9, 10, 11, 35
Velasco, Fernando de, 7, 8
Velez, 53
Vetancurt, Agustín de, 5, 22, 68, 70, 73
Villa-Señor y Sánchez, José A., 69, 73
Vivian, Gordon, 70, 73

Walpi, 13
Wilson, Frank, ix
Witkind, William B., ix, xiii, xiv, 9, 20,
  21, 22, 35, 40, 43, 45, 46, 48, 51, 58
Woodbury, Natalie F., 70, 72
Woodbury, Richard B., 70, 72

Ye, Juan de, 9

Zambrano Ortiz, Pedro, 2, 4, 19
Zárate Salmerón, Gerónimo de, 5
Zeinos, Diego de la Casa, 9, 12, 16, 35,
  40, 42, 48, 50